ARMOR

ATTAIN
EMOTIONAL FREEDOM BY
RESOLVING ISSUES FROM CHILDHOOD

Debbie Wallace

Copyright © 2021 by Debbie Wallace

All rights reserved. Contents and/or cover may not be reproduced in whole or in part in any form without the express written consent of the publisher.

ISBNs: 978-1-7369039-0-2(pbk); 978-1-7369039-1-9 (kindle)
Library of Congress Control Number: 2021905804

Unless otherwise noted, all scripture quotations are taken from THE HOLY BIBLE, ENGLISH STANDARD VERSION. esv® Text Edition: 2016. Copyright © 2001 by Crossway Bibles, a publishing ministry of Good News Publishers. Used by permission.

Scripture quotations marked (NIV) are taken from the HOLY BIBLE, NEW INTERNATIONAL VERSION®, NIV®. Copyright © 1973, 1978, 1984, 2011 by Biblica, Inc.™ Used by permission of Zondervan.

Scripture quotations marked (NKJV) are taken from the New King James Version of the Bible. Copyright © 1979, 1980, 1982, Thomas Nelson, Inc., Publishers. Used by permission. All rights reserved.

Scripture quotations marked (KJV) are taken from the KING JAMES VERSION, public domain.

Cover and layout: Mayfly Design

Published by Peace Lily Publishing
PO Box 11984
Jackson TN 38308
www.peacelilypublishing.com

Printed in the United States of America.

*To my three lovely daughters
Summer, Shay, and Shannon*

CONTENTS

Introduction — vii

PART 1: THE HEART BONDAGE

CHAPTER ONE: Brokenness and Breakthrough — 3
CHAPTER TWO: It's All About the Heart — 19
CHAPTER THREE: Understanding Spiritual Bondage — 33
CHAPTER FOUR: How a Heart Bondage Works — 49
CHAPTER FIVE: Serious Symptoms — 59
CHAPTER SIX: Types of Strongholds — 71
CHAPTER SEVEN: Scriptural Foundation — 79
CHAPTER EIGHT: The Truth Encounter — 91

PART 2: THE JOURNEY

CHAPTER NINE: The Power of a Testimony — 105
CHAPTER TEN: The Full Armor of God — 117
CHAPTER ELEVEN: The Kingdom of God — 127
CHAPTER TWELVE: The Power of Choice — 137
CHAPTER THIRTEEN: A Measure of Grace — 147
CHAPTER FOURTEEN: The Freedom Class Online — 155

Acknowledgments — 159
About the Author — 161
Preview Instead of Disgrace — 163

*Instead of your shame
you will receive a double portion,*

*And instead of disgrace
you will rejoice in your inheritance.*

*And so you will inherit a double portion
in your land,*

*And everlasting joy
will be yours.*

—Isaiah 61:7 (NIV)

INTRODUCTION

I INVITE YOU ON A JOURNEY THAT COULD VERY POSSIBLY change your life. Such a journey certainly changed mine—and I needed change, because there was a time when I was desperately ashamed to be me. Not because I had done anything to be ashamed of particularly—but because I was *convinced,* totally convinced that I did not matter. But God set me free from the bondage of shame and hopelessness, and that is how I became a teacher and proponent of radical emotional freedom.

I must admit I was a most unlikely candidate for a deliverance. Raised in a two-parent home with a strong family background in ministry, it would appear that I had no excuse. My parents loved each other, they provided for my needs, and we attended church every time the doors were open. By the time I was twelve, I was playing the piano in church services. I always sensed an anointing on my life. No one—and I mean *no one*—would have suspected that I suffered from a debilitating sense of shattered self-worth.

How this came to be is a scene as old as time. When I was eight years old, some words were spoken that reshaped my identity and made me ashamed of who I believed myself to be. Some other unfortunate experiences followed—poverty, for one, and the mental illness of a parent—and soon I knew of a certainty that I was a nobody and a nothing. To compound matters, I believed in my heart of hearts that nothing I could ever do would change that.

Going away to college provided a ray of hope. I wanted to escape to freedom and a new life—yet within just a few weeks, those old familiar feelings of shame and unworthiness reemerged. Convinced there was no way out, I thought my only option was to work with the brokenness.

So I created a facade of success and happiness that would hide my broken identity behind well-laid plans of accomplishment, prosperity, and education. *As long as no one knows*, I thought. *As long as no one knows who I really am.*

The story that follows is almost humorous in its complexity. It's the tale of how one competent-yet-broken person attempted to caulk the cracks of her shattered existence just enough to cover her insecurities. But the shame talked, and it led to a life of hardship and hopelessness where verbal and emotional abuse were the norm. This is a true story, and thankfully one with a happy ending—but the story is not really just my story. Fact is, it's very possibly *your story too.*

There is a familiar pattern in the lives of those whose minds have been shaped by unworthiness. All our stories seem to run along the same course, converging upon our respective identities in fear and confusion. How we each respond to emotional pain may vary, but respond we must, and our personal narratives almost always involve some form of self-destruction. So when you hear me tell of how I married a man with narcissistic traits, whose mother was also a controller, and how the verbal and emotional abuse were so severe that I could only survive the pain by lying to myself daily, perhaps you will understand.

And when I admit that I questioned God, and even at times suspected He was in on the plan to destroy my life, maybe you'll relate with that as well. When we cannot handle the truth—that we have failed to respond to the accusations of shame in a constructive manner—we look for someone else to share our self-blame. As my life fell apart, I cried out to the Lord, "Why have You allowed all of these things to happen to me?"

Thank God, He is never offended by our honesty. Or our misguided desperation.

And when I express how I grieved in the fact that no one came to my rescue, perhaps you'll know what I mean. I walked away from God and church for five years, out of sheer frustration. But at the end of that time, defeated by shame and with my life burned to the ground, I renewed my relationship with Jesus Christ. There was simply nowhere else to go. As you might say, *I surrendered.*

Now that may be the end of the similarities between our stories.

(I hope not.) But for the first time, this believer truly gave her heart to Jesus. I repented, and then I did something else: I made the declaration to trust God (something I had never done before)—and suddenly *everything changed*. My thought patterns, my attitudes, my preconceived ideas, beliefs, and assumptions began to evolve. I reconciled my thinking to His one step at a time; and through that process, the Lord literally walked me out of the past. I connected with my identity in Christ—with who God says I am. I discovered my right to be me and not be ashamed or without hope in life. In short, Jesus Christ set me free!

After my freedom experience, my heart burned with compassion for those shackled with the burden of shame and hopelessness. Shame is a wicked tool of deception the devil uses to undermine people's confidence. It's an attempt to prevent them from ever comprehending their true identity—who God says they are.

I like to believe if someone had offered me a way out of my brokenness at age eighteen, I would have jumped at the chance. As a college freshman who keenly recognized the presence of a spiritual heaviness on my life, I longed for answers that took me decades to find.

But find them I did. Only by the Holy Spirit's guidance, the goodness of a gracious God, and the blood of Jesus Christ could I receive the kind of radical, liberating freedom that changes lives. And not only did I gain my freedom, I was able to look back and comprehend the measures that took me there. With that discovery came a fierce passion that was born of a divine calling: *sharing my journey with others so they can receive their freedom as well*. I knew my deliverance was not just for me.

On the morning I received my freedom, a dream stepped up to the plate. It wasn't a new dream, but one that had been with me all my life—a dream that had been stirred occasionally through various words of personal prophecy and revealed from time to time in quick glimpses of a distant future. Though I always felt the promptings of a divine calling, the dream had elusively evaded capture. On that day however, the dream made itself known. I understood it.

A divine calling is not like any other dream. Ordinary dreams may fade, but when God calls a person, nothing can deter the pursuit of that dream or dim the brilliance of the anointing. No amount of discouragement, difficulty, complications, or—the big one, the passage of time—

can unravel the call. Even if one never answers the call of God, it stands. It's a divine assignment, and the Lord never changes His mind.

Leading others to emotional freedom is my purpose, my calling, and my challenge. In engaging that challenge, I will start here by giving you a promise *to be faithful to that calling and present to you God's way of setting people free*—unfiltered, unmodified, and undiminished. I'm giving it to you straight.

In this book I will give you my story. I will describe emotional bondage in vivid detail. You'll be amazed as you discover the source of so much pain and confusion, the origin of dysfunction and chaos. As one of my students said, "That answers a lot of questions."

I will then discuss the best way to go about seeking emotional freedom, and you'll receive an invitation to join me in The Freedom Class, an online classroom I created to bring God's truth and freedom to others. You will have the opportunity to deal with any issues from your childhood, walk away from the shadows of your past, and claim a lasting victory over your life.

The process that leads to emotional freedom is so simple you could miss it. It's an effective course outlined in the Bible for "pulling down strongholds"—a time-tested, often practical solution that works for anyone willing to renew their faith, take the risk of change, and believe that God *not only can but will set you free*. Nothing is complicated about it. I assure you, if I could do it, you can too.

The course presented in this book and the subsequent volumes that comprise The Armor Series is not my own invention, not my process, but a biblical one. I am simply passing on to you what God did for me. That's why The Freedom Class is a path to lasting emotional freedom. Once you get free, you can stay free. You won't have to worry about becoming enslaved again to any old chains of bondage. Because when Jesus Christ sets you free, you'll be "free indeed"!

It's *God's way of doing things.*

PART 1

THE HEART BONDAGE

CHAPTER ONE

Brokenness and Breakthrough

I WOULD CALL IT *SHAME*. SHAME IS FEELING BAD BECAUSE of who you are—as opposed to guilt, which is feeling bad for something you may have done. The fetters of shame are often associated with people who have been sexually molested or physically abused, or those who have experienced horrific childhood trauma. I didn't have that kind of history.

I came from a two-parent home, and my parents loved each other. We were poor, but no one seemed to fret about it much. I had an older brother and a younger sister. We lived in the country, and we stayed home most of the time, so we didn't have much of a social life.

With a strong family background in ministry, my family was moral to a fault. We attended church on Sunday morning, Sunday evening, Wednesday evening, and any special services that might present an opportunity to worship in the little country church where I spent so much of my childhood. I was a musically gifted child and, by the time I was twelve, I regularly played the piano in church services. I always had a heart for God and loved to serve Him. Even at a young age, I sensed an anointing on my life.

But when I was eight years old something happened that made an indelible mark on my mind. It was a cold January day, and I had just come home from school. We had recently moved from Texas back to South Arkansas where my mother grew up, so I was the new kid at school. I got off the school bus at my grandparents' house that afternoon, excited about the possibilities of new friendships. I began telling my mom all about my new friends when she interrupted me. Looking me straight in the eye, she told me the people in our community didn't think our family was as "good" as they were. She said I could play with the other children at school, but I needed to understand that they would never accept me.

I didn't know what to say; in fact, there was nothing I could say. I was crushed. I stole away to a quiet part of the house to be alone. Sitting on the edge of my grandparents' bed, I tried to recover from the shock, but it seemed the room was reeling. I slowly contemplated this dreadful news about who I was—or wasn't—as my mother's words began to sink in. I can still hear the silence in that room.

I remember thinking I didn't believe what she said was true but somehow it became true, because she was my mother, and she believed it. For some reason I didn't understand, she had the authority to make it true because she had spoken it over me. It became as she had said.

A sadness overcame me, a dreadful heaviness. When I went back to school the next day, I couldn't look the other children in the eye. I was ashamed. I was so ashamed to be me.

Immediately I began building up walls around my heart. I didn't realize I was building anything like walls, but I surely was; and within a short time, those internal defenses were impenetrable. My self-worth was severely damaged. Outwardly I could appear bright and outgoing; but on the inside, those walls were a steel fortress. They protected that shameful place from exposure and created a barrier to keep others out. Without a doubt, I knew I was a nothing and a nobody, and I didn't matter.

To compound the issues I had concerning my intrinsic value, I wrestled with the daily struggle of living with a mentally ill parent. My mother was diagnosed as bipolar and was so severely crippled by depression that many days she could not function. Her good days were very high, and her bad days were very low. And the two were so erratic that no one ever knew what to expect from one day to the next. To ease the tension, I began creating "happy" situations to help steer her into having a good day. I tried to make things pleasant so she wouldn't plunge into depression as soon as she walked out of her bedroom. I didn't know then the meaning of *codependency*, but I had become an enabler to her dysfunction. I was forming relationship habits that would come back to haunt me later.

My mother's illness stretched throughout my teen years and beyond. Her dark days were frequent, but on her good days, she appeared almost normal like any other mom. As time passed, however, she became more controlling. My father was disabled, and the poverty was grueling. I never blamed my parents. I honestly felt then, as I do now, that they did the best they could. Interestingly, I never told anyone what it was like for me at home. I never spoke a word, but I secretly harbored one single hope: "If I can ever just grow up . . ."

Finally, I did grow up. As a new high school graduate, I went away to college. With great expectations, I moved into the dorm that September fully prepared to live my best life. Escaping the negative influences of home was a huge relief, though I felt guilty for leaving. But I knew all too well that I could never resolve the difficulties back home, and this was my chance to gain my freedom and begin to live life the way I had dreamed. I had high hopes! I was a good student, I made friends quickly, and I was ready to shake off that old heaviness. It didn't take long for me to realize that wasn't going to happen.

Something was wrong. I had been at school only a few weeks when I became aware of the tug of those old familiar feelings of shame and unworthiness. I felt I was dragging a ball and chain. I knew I was pretty, smart, and capable—at least as much as any other girl. But I had no hope. My whole life was before me, yet nothing had changed. The fresh opportunities of my new life couldn't silence the old convictions of my heart—that I was still a nothing and a nobody, and I didn't matter. And I was absolutely certain that could never be changed.

I had assumed that if I could escape my childhood environment, I could escape from the heaviness and the shame. But whatever had affected me back home followed me to college. It wasn't about my environment or my geographic location, it was about me. And it wasn't just *about* me, but rather it *was* me. *It was me!* I tried not to panic as the alarming sensation struck me that this condition was permanent.

I wasn't exactly sure what to call this condition. For lack of a better term, I called it a "self-esteem" problem. That made me feel a little better because I'd read about self-esteem, and I knew lots of people

> **The main thing was to keep anyone else from finding out. I thought I had to hide the real me because I believed the real me was flawed.**

struggle with that. But I wasn't going to just give up. I wasn't going to take it lying down. Not me! I determined to beat this thing somehow.

So when I realized I was stuck with the ball and chain—whatever it was—I decided I would outperform it. I would succeed! I would work harder than everybody else and try to be really good at everything I did. I would play the piano better, and sing better, and dress better, and make more friends, and make more money, and I would put on a big smile so no one would ever know . . . that I was ashamed. That I was a nothing and a nobody. *That I didn't matter.*

The main thing was to keep anyone else from finding out. I thought I had to hide the real me because I believed the real me was flawed. To make my life work, I needed to appear to be the kind of person others would accept. I was convinced that faking it was the solution—*the only solution* to my dilemma. Although I was a genuine person at heart, I thought I had no choice. And that is how I constructed a facade of success and happiness that would fool pretty much anybody.

Several years later, I graduated from college. I had done an excellent job of keeping up the facade, which had become second nature by then. I had a great time during those college years, and I made many friends. In short, my plan was working. Then several years after college graduation, an amazing thing happened: I married a man who turned out to be very much a controller! (He had all the characteristics of a *narcissist*, although I didn't know the meaning of that term at the time.) He was an only child, and his mother was a controller as well.

Heartache and pain followed. The verbal and emotional abuse started at a relatively moderate level, but before long became entirely out of control. The criticism was vicious, the demands unyielding, the threats excessive—and all part of daily life. I made excuses for the behavior of these people, taking on the responsibility of making everyone happy and trying to solve all their problems.

Once again, I became the enabler. I began creating happy situations to keep things pleasant, many times at my own expense. The dysfunction I was conditioned to tolerate as a teen was venting its anger on me once more. I honestly believed I deserved it. And of course, I never forgot that I didn't matter anyway.

Before long, I was in way over my head. Overwhelmed and afraid, I fought to keep up appearances. I kept working hard to be successful at everything I did. I kept the facade, I kept the smile, and I never talked about it to anyone. Not one single person on the face of the earth ever knew what was going on in my head or behind the closed doors of my wrecked life. I desperately wanted to believe that if I could pretend the situation wasn't that bad, and if I could paint the pretty picture I wanted everyone to see, then perhaps everything would turn out all right eventually. And that was my goal—to make it all work out.

I sincerely wanted to resolve these difficulties, and I thought I could, if I just didn't quit. The problem was, my heart was taking a beating. I wasn't black and blue physically, but emotionally I was being destroyed. I would go to bed at night with a knot in my stomach, knowing what I would have to face the next day—and face it I did. Because it never stopped. These people in my life—these authority figures—sought day by day to manipulate me through verbal and emotional abuse. It was heartless, relentless, and brutal.

Outside the influence of the controllers, I did find some happiness. I had many great friends, and I did well as a realtor. The brightest spot in my life was my children—three delightful daughters (a blonde, a brunette, and a redhead!) who were the light of my life. My love for those three little girls was the reason I was able to face each day and keep going.

We attended a wonderful local church with a great children's ministry, and I was the praise and worship leader there for some years. All my girls were active in school events, and they were also involved in church activities. I was committed to raising my children right.

The time came when I began to collapse under the weight of the emotional strain. About the time my girls entered their teens, that facade of success began to crack. I could feel a deep-seated anger beginning to rise up in me, and I began to despise the controllers. I stopped making excuses for them. I was furious with them because of what they had done to me. Instead of getting better, the abuse had escalated as they returned my love with contempt and my kindness with cruelty. I questioned God, and I began to be angry with Him too. I didn't want to be angry and bitter, but I didn't know what else to think.

I had submitted to authority, I had served God faithfully, I had done the "right thing," and I had gotten badly hurt—steamrolled, in fact. I had come to realize I didn't deserve that kind of abuse; I had never deserved it and, at that juncture, I didn't know how to make heads or tails of the mess that was my life. Something had gone wrong somewhere, but I had trouble reconciling that raw reality with my attitudes, convictions, and efforts. I was so confused. I had tried so hard! *How could anyone who had tried so hard fail so completely?*

But failure is precisely what I was looking at. No longer willing to allow the controllers to work their self-indulgences through me, no longer yielding to their criticism, I began to fight back, and things started falling apart. The years had passed. All three of my beautiful daughters, now young adults, were rebelling. My finances flatlined as my body weight soared, and my career appeared to be all but over. In this setting, a series of events quite effectively demolished the rest of my life's efforts—like a hurricane, a tornado, and a tsunami all at the same time. I think I felt a little like Job.

I had nowhere to turn. Disappointed with everything and everybody, all my dreams shattered, I realized with an increasing sense of dread that my resources for recouping were dwindling as each year passed. My life was burning to the ground, and I was powerless to stop it. I wondered how God could stand idly by day after day, month after month, while the months rolled into years, allowing me to get beaten up by bullies—controllers—people I was supposed to "submit" to. (How I had come to hate that word!) Didn't He understand that if I saw one of my daughters getting pushed around, I would step in and start swinging if I had to? Why wouldn't He do that for me? Where had He been during all this time? We're talking about a lifetime of pain.

God, why have You allowed all this to happen to me? I knew I would

>
> *I had to admit to myself that I could not fix my life. I couldn't fix myself, I couldn't fix the controllers, I couldn't fix anything. That I'd ever thought I could suddenly appeared to me as sheer foolishness.*

always love God, but I could not locate His love for me. It appeared that He was passive toward me. It seemed I just didn't matter to Him, and I didn't understand it. I had served Him for so long, and yet He was silent to my cry. He seemed remote, a million miles away. In my hopelessness, I grieved in the hard fact that the Lord had waited so long to help me. So much time had passed! Even if He did eventually come to my rescue, wouldn't it be too late?

I withdrew from serving God. For five long years, I stopped going to church (and for me, that was a big deal). I wanted God to come find me and rescue me, to tell me He loved me. I felt I was staring at God, questioning. Waiting for some kind of answer, some word of explanation, anything—but there was nothing. Just empty silence. I did hear a voice, however, a voice from my past. It was an accusing voice, and it told me again what had been so painful for me to hear all through the years: *See, you really don't matter . . . You don't even matter to God.*

Then one day I hit bottom. This magnificent event occurred on a quiet Sunday afternoon, during a Fourth of July weekend, as I was working in my laundry room. Through a small, insignificant incident, my eyes were opened, and I had to admit to myself that I could not fix my life. I couldn't fix myself, I couldn't fix the controllers, I couldn't fix anything. That I'd ever thought I could suddenly appeared to me as sheer foolishness. I had to acknowledge I had been lying to myself because I didn't want to see the truth. I had ignored hard evidence that was right in front of me so I could hold onto what I wanted to believe: that I could create a beautiful life through my own efforts and make myself into the kind of person others would accept. So I made a decision for truth that day. I pledged never to lie to myself again, ever. About anything.

At that same moment, I made a decision to renew my relationship with Jesus Christ. I decided to stop worrying about whether or not I was important to God; He was important to me. I wasn't at all sure that God loved me as much as He loved others, but I couldn't worry about that anymore, and I couldn't be mad at Him anymore either. I've always had a supernatural love for God, and I was so hungry for His presence. I just wanted to worship with His people. So I made yet another decision—to go back to church. I would serve God regardless, no matter what. Once I made that commitment, I never missed a beat. Soon I was serving on the praise team, playing the keyboard again.

Several months passed. Except for my attitude, not much in my life had changed since that day in my laundry room. I was uncertain about my future, which looked a lot like a black hole. But I kept putting one foot in front of the other. Life was different for me now, because I refused to lie to myself anymore—although I was still dealing with my ugly facts. The landscape of my life appeared to be just a heap of ashes. However, I no longer allowed myself to view my circumstances through rose-colored glasses. I refused to make excuses for anything or anybody. I was trying to go forward, but much of the time I felt I was tripping over all the baggage. That intense anger was still with me, and I fought daily to keep it from consuming me.

One Sunday morning, my pastor spoke in a sermon about trusting God. His honesty touched me. He said because of a tragedy that occurred in his teens, he'd lived for years knowing that he didn't trust God, even while serving as pastor. He shared how he finally did reach a place of trust through God's grace and mercy. His admission struck a chord in me. It made me feel a little less ashamed of what I already knew—that I didn't trust God. I had tried to convince myself that God is good like everybody says, but to me, it just didn't add up. My life experiences did not paint a reassuring picture of the Lord, and I had to be honest. I saw God as a God of judgment, not a God of love.

I went home that Sunday afternoon, still thinking about the pastor's story. I planned to take a nap because I'd recently begun working at night, and I had to get some sleep. As I laid my head on the pillow, I whispered, "God, I wish I could trust You." Immediately I heard the words, *"Can I trust you?"*

Speechless. I was speechless. God had spoken to me! I had finally heard God again, and it was specific—that is, I heard the exact words, not just an impression. I heard it plainly, so clearly that it might have been considered audible. (I would describe it as telepathy.) Hearing from God meant that He was there, that He had been there all along. It meant that He was aware, and He had not forgotten me. A fleeting revolutionary thought struck me that perhaps I'd been wrong, that maybe I did matter to Him after all. Maybe I had been too eager to entangle God with my own mistakes.

I knew exactly what God wanted: He wanted me to trust Him, to make a declaration to that effect. Somehow I understood I would go no further until I did so. Also, the Lord's question to me—*Can I trust you?*—implied I had not been faithful. That question was a challenge. I saw that it was time to do some real soul-searching, to take a long, hard look in the mirror, because the weight of responsibility was swinging in my direction, and I wasn't about to run from it.

Now this was a big jump. Just the thought of trusting God was tough for me because of my experiences with the authority figures in my life. I had never really trusted anybody, and I was seriously afraid of God. However, this trust challenge was thrown down by none other than the Lord Himself—*how could I say no?*—and I decided to take that leap. It would be a stretch, but I knew I would do it. God had gone to the trouble to make Himself known to me in my disappointment, so I decided right then and there to risk it all. So I made the declaration.

Aloud, I said, "Okay, God, I trust You. I decide to trust You." Immediately I went to sleep. When I awoke later that night to go to work, I felt a tingling expectancy in the room, almost as if the atmosphere was charged. For the first time, I seriously suspected that God might be up to something.

About this time, I had begun praying every morning at 3:00 a.m. I was working nights, so I was up at all hours anyway. But there seemed to be something special about that 3:00 a.m. prayer, during which time some things began to move around in me. Especially after I made the decision to trust, there was a marked change. My perspectives began to shift—totally unexpected on my part—as I started to view things differently, and many burdens lifted off me through no effort of my own.

The Lord began to do some housework in my heart. Much of this

Brokenness and Breakthrough

involved repentance, but not necessarily as one might expect. Most of the time it was about past situations I wouldn't have considered sinful at all. Sometimes I hadn't exactly done anything wrong, yet God showed me how my thought processes had been in error. He repeatedly took me back to specific occasions in my past, some years and even decades earlier, and led me to see where, time after time, I had been upside-down in my thinking. I had been defensive, viewing life through the eyes of brokenness. But through His gentle correction, the Lord helped me to see why my perspectives were off, and what a healthy perspective would look like in each situation. The Holy Spirit was reteaching me how to think.

Though I had viewed my problems as external (the controllers), God wasn't dealing with that. Instead, He was rearranging things *in me*. It wasn't my actions He was correcting as much as my heart—the way I perceived life: my thought patterns, my attitudes, my preconceived notions, my unfounded beliefs and assumptions. As the Lord corrected my thinking in each situation, I listened with the ears of my heart as hard as I could, and I never argued with Him about anything. I took His every correction and adjustment with gratitude, and I genuinely repented in each instance. I made sure I reconciled my thinking to His as He directed me.

As I complied with the Lord's corrections, He made permanent adjustments in my heart, and my perspectives kept changing. God was correcting my thought processes, which were so damaged as a child. He was effectively walking me out of the past.

These God-corrections came one at a time. The Lord waited for me to get each one right before He moved on to the next lesson. Soon I saw that one completed lesson would open the door to a new one. I understood that it was essential to be explicitly obedient. I had to get the lesson, accept the correction, repent, and gratefully receive the attitude adjustment before we could proceed to the next God-correction. I absorbed the Lord's gentle corrections like a sponge. For someone who'd been trying to get it right for decades, learning life lessons from the Giver of life was the ultimate in solutions. When I figured out how God worked, I began to respond faster. Soon I was responding daily.

We began moving fast. I had the sensation that my spirit was running. I wasn't sure exactly where God was leading me, but I knew we

> *God was correcting my thought processes, which were so damaged as a child. He was effectively walking me out of the past.*

were going somewhere. I had decided to trust Him, so wherever we were going, I wanted to get there as quickly as possible. I found I liked this trusting God thing, and I wasn't looking back.

Then one evening, something began to happen. Toward the end of a Wednesday evening church service, our praise leader began to sing "I Surrender All." Standing at my keyboard across the platform, I couldn't stop the tears. For the first time ever, I was able to sing that song from my heart. I had been a Christian all my life, brought up in the church—had even been a leader in the churches I attended and had been sincere in it. I had been the walking definition of faithful. I had sung "I Surrender All" countless times, but I had never truly surrendered to Him, nor had I even understood what that meant. I had been so determined that I was not going to fail.

I had believed if I were patient enough and loved the controllers enough, they would finally get it. I thought if I just didn't quit, it would all work out; if I worked a little harder, it would all come together. But finally, faced with utter failure on all fronts, disappointed to the core, with no hope in sight and nowhere else to turn, I was forced to look to Jesus. And in doing so, I had arrived at the place where He'd wanted me all along: *the place of surrender.*

A few hours later, I was at work. The clock said 2:30 a.m., just a half-hour before my scheduled prayer time. Caught up on my duties, I thought I'd listen to a quick video, so I clicked on a sermon by Bishop T. D. Jakes: "If You Want to See a Move of God." The video started, and Bishop Jakes was already in the middle of his sermon. He was under a heavy anointing, and he said: "If you want to see a move of God, you'll quit messing with these folks that haven't been through anything." Suddenly I was locked onto his words. My feet were rooted to the floor, my eyes glued to the screen. It seemed my heart had stopped. He continued,

Brokenness and Breakthrough

"If you really want to see the anointing flow, you have to have somebody who has been *crushed*."

Then—at that moment, *right there,* an understanding instantly swept over me. I got it. And every chain, every device of bondage the enemy could ever use to shackle a little girl of eight years old, fell to my feet. I felt it over my entire being—a pulse, a quick invisible flash—*a pop.* I was stunned. Tears sprang to my eyes, and I knew. I knew! *Yes!!!* This is what is called *being set free!* I felt I could soar. The relief was incredible.

You can probably imagine what my prayer time was like that morning. Thankful, so thankful, I could only vacillate between sobs and laughter. Where there had been sorrow, now there was joy. Where there was disappointment, now was hope. Where there was confusion, now understanding. I saw that God had been there all along, with a divine plan that gave my suffering significance and purpose. I found that God really is good, and He truly does love me. He loves me! And God is faithful. He never gave up on me. The flames of shame had all but destroyed me, but even as my life lay in ruins, He saw me as worth saving. I knew He would help me go forward.

In the days and weeks following my deliverance, I felt I was *walking out* of the bondage. The chains no longer held me captive, yet they were nearby. I sensed they were lying at my feet. I had the extraordinary opportunity to step over them and walk away. I was free, but I had to train my mind to be free. Thinking and acting like a free person was no longer difficult, but it was not something that came naturally either. I had to practice freedom until it became second nature.

My thought processes continued to change and evolve over the coming weeks, even months. I discovered a love and respect for myself which I had not known before. I felt lighter. Eventually, the wounds in my heart healed. And that is how, over time, I was able to experience yet another miracle: that of being *made whole,* which is the inner healing that follows emotional deliverance. I was whole, finally! I joyfully connected with my true identity in Christ—who God says I am—and I learned to exercise my own personal authority. With gratitude and delight, I discovered the right *just to be me.*

And I was not ashamed.

CHAPTER ONE WORKBOOK

BROKENNESS AND BREAKTHROUGH

How to Write Your Testimony

Your first Workbook assignment is to write your testimony. Condensing your life history into a short story that others can read in a matter of minutes requires a bit of courage, some humility, and a heavy hand on the editing. Keep it simple and honest.

Take your time as you write your story. I don't suggest that you try to finish this project in one day, one week, or even one month. You certainly don't have to complete this assignment before continuing on to the next chapter. But allow yourself time for insight and reflection as you record your story, even as it continues to unfold. Your testimony an ongoing effort, subject to updates at any point in time.

The rules:

1. Start with your childhood and continue in chronological order of events. In this study, the focus is on childhood concerns. While you will want to touch on all the high points (and low ones too) of your entire life up to now, be sure to include your early years and the events which impacted your emotions, attitudes, and perceptions as a child.

2. Do not concentrate on feelings. Don't get hung up on disclosing all the details or expounding excessively on how you felt about an experience. A simple statement about what happened and how you reacted is sufficient.

3. Try not to throw anyone under the bus. Respect others' privacy, even if they have caused you tremendous hardship and pain. If you must

state facts that put others in a bad light, you may wish to change the abuser's name or relation to you—or perhaps not. Protect your own privacy as well.

4. Focus on yourself. For example, another way to say, "My father abandoned me when I was in first grade," might be, "I grew up in a single-parent household."

5. Write about what mattered. Give attention to those events and circumstances that made a mark, like turning points in time.

6. Use discretion concerning delicate situations. You do not need to describe the details of certain traumatic events, such as sexual abuse. You don't need to explain everything to the reader. This is just for you and will only be shared if you want to share it.

7. Be real. Be as genuine and transparent as you can.

I'm convinced that the best way to write your story is simply to begin. You don't have to be a great writer to write your testimony. Even if you're naturally good at writing and journaling, the following list can be used as a starting point to help you write your story. Add all information that you feel is important.

1. Where were you born?

2. Tell about your family. Did you have both parents? Were your parents married, divorced? How many brothers and sisters did you have, and what was the birth order? If you didn't have a family, then tell about that.

3. Where did you live? City or country, apartment or house? Did you move around a lot?

4. Describe your home life.

5. Tell about your mom's personality. What about your dad's?

6. How did you relate to your mom and dad? The rest of your family? How did you feel about your family?

7. Where did you go to school? What kind of student were you? How did you interact with your classmates? Were you studious? Adventurous?

8. Tell about the economics in your home growing up. Was your family rich, poor, or somewhere in between? Were your needs met?

9. Was spirituality part of your childhood? Did you go to church? What kind of relationship with God did you have as a child and teenager?

10. Tell about your friends. Did you make friends easily, have few friends, were you a loner? Did you have a lot of peer pressure, and how did you respond?

11. What subjects interested you in school? Did you excel in anything? Sports? Music? Math?

12. What was important to your family? What did your family do together for fun? What were they known for in the community? If you say "nothing," that is fine.

13. What was important to you? What were your dreams growing up?

14. Was there a traumatic event or adverse childhood experience that changed you? Did it reoccur? (If not a specific event, was there a prevailing condition?) How did you respond?

15. How did you react when bad things happened to you? Did you experience abuse, neglect, or adverse childhood conditions? How did you cope with situations that were out of your control?

16. Describe your teen years. Who/what was your most significant influence during that time?

17. What did you do after high school? What were your plans for your life?

18. What did you value the most as a young adult? Education, establishing a career, travel, romance? Starting a family? Partying? Money? Cars, boats, etc.? Feeling important? Ministry? Helping others?

19. Describe your relationships throughout your adult life. Did you relate well with others? Were you needy? Did you feel you were being controlled or in control? Did you think other people liked you? Were you angry? Afraid? Outgoing? Shy?

20. Did you develop any habits or destructive behaviors that you could not seem to break? (Chemical dependencies, promiscuous behavior, serving as a doormat for others, chronic lying, criminal behavior, etc.)

21. What were the major turning points in your life, in your childhood?

22. What has God done for you so far?

23. Where are you in your life now? What are your greatest successes? What are your greatest frustrations? What is your greatest hope?

24. Describe your current relationship with Jesus Christ.

25. What do you see for your future? How did your past help to create a path for your future?

After each chapter, I offer some workbook questions to help review the key points from the chapter. You may find it useful to reread your testimony from time to time and review the progress you're making there, in relation to the workbook questions. I suggest creating a separate journal or notebook where you can share your thoughts freely and think about the questions. Ask God to guide you in this journey and you can be assured that He will be with you every step of the way.

CHAPTER TWO

It's All About the Heart

THE PRIMARY FOCUS OF THIS DISCUSSION IS TO EXAMine the condition of the heart. Not the physical heart, of course, but the heart of the soul. The heart is often spoken of figuratively and serves as a reference for that which feels deeply. The heart is the domain of inspiration and creativity, the seat of all emotion. We have heard it said, "It came from my heart," or, "My heart is full of compassion." The Bible speaks of the heart numerous times.

> *Above all else, guard your heart,*
> *for everything you do flows from it.*
> *—Proverbs 4:23 (NIV)*

In this verse, the word *heart* is interpreted as "inner man" or "midst." Hebrew culture has always understood the heart to incorporate *the mind, the will, and the emotions,* including all thought processes. While traditional thought might assign the ability to think strictly to the brain, and emotion to the heart, we know that the heart definitely includes the brain and all thought processes, and also embodies the emotions, the conscience, and the will. The heart is the sphere that comprises the whole of the inner person.

Our Creator designed the heart and soul in all its intricate detail. According to God's Word, all people—male and female—were created in God's image (Genesis 1:27). In a sense, we are all cut from the same pattern. With that in mind, it's easy to see how the human heart follows a particular path. Whether you are loved unconditionally or emotionally injured, the heart will respond. It's not entirely that simple, considering various personality types, gender differences, birth order, culture, and life experiences—but the heart will respond. The heart can lay hold of the concepts of right and wrong even at an early age. Love, respect, fairness, and equality register on the human heart. The heart also understands when those things have been violated. You don't have to tell a child when they have been defiled. They know.

Whole vs. Broken

A secure, positive environment is a great beginning for boys and girls. Children have a better chance of developing to their full potential as adults if they receive a healthy amount of the classic childhood elements: love, education, guidance, encouragement, and discipline. We might call this adult child a *whole person*. But what about that little boy or girl who has a different kind of childhood? Many children have had this experience. I had that other kind of childhood.

By this admission, I don't mean that my parents didn't care for me properly or that they were terrible people. Actually, I had very good parents. They loved me and frequently told me so. They provided for my material and educational needs and raised me to serve God. We were faithful about attending church. There was a lot I never saw growing up, such as alcohol and drug abuse or physical violence. My mom and dad worked hard, instructed me to respect authority, and taught me good manners. And yet I still ended up with chains on my heart.

Dealing with issues from childhood doesn't require that you disrespect your family. God's Word says we should honor our parents. We can do that even as we acknowledge that our parents were not perfect. It's important to recognize that we are not going to hate on our parents or anyone else in this examination. This is not a blame game. But to make sure we're on the same page, let me state here and now that *this discussion*

> **This discussion is not about our parents.** *It's not about our grandparents, our relatives, or any other authority figures from our past.* **It's about you and me.**

is not about our parents. It's not about our grandparents, our relatives, or any other authority figures from our past. *It's about you and me.*

Acknowledging that we experienced a degree of trauma during childhood doesn't necessarily mean we experienced abuse, although we may have. It doesn't automatically mean our parents didn't take their responsibilities seriously or that our family is the standard of dysfunction, although they may be. It doesn't even have to mean anyone intentionally harmed us. What it does mean is that something happened that shaped our life in a negative way. At some point, usually at a young age, an indelible mark was made upon our mind.

Anyone sexually molested in childhood will feel the psychological impact of that abuse as a child and into adulthood. The same is true for those who witnessed or suffered physical violence or verbal or emotional cruelty. A child with an alcoholic or substance-dependent parent will suffer the long-term effects of trauma, as will those with a mentally ill parent. Excessive bickering and fighting between parents or family members will subject a child to brokenness, especially if it involves verbal or physical violence. But often a negative impact is made on the mind of a child through seemingly ordinary situations that are less than traumatic. Less than obvious. It doesn't have to look like abuse at all.

Constant criticism, accusation, excessive control, manipulation, and nagging can damage a child's heart, as can the practice of preferring one child over another. Refusing a child the opportunity to develop their natural gifts—such as leadership, creativity, or music—can often sustain an injury to the heart. Considerable poverty is often a catalyst for brokenness and is one of the most common conditions for creating emotional bondage. Damaging words, even well meant, can make an impact that lasts a lifetime.

Often heart issues arise because one or both parents are not fully

It's All About the Heart **21**

present, and the child feels a sense of abandonment. There can be an unmet need in the child raised by a single parent, even when the parent does the best he or she can. This same need is often felt by those left with a grandparent or relative out of necessity. Even if both parents are present in the home, a sense of abandonment can still emerge if one parent does not bond with the child.

Neglecting to express love to a child or refusing to take the time to build quality relationships within the family can initiate emotional distress. A home environment where Mom or Dad is a workaholic also qualifies. Well-meaning parents who work excessive hours, whether out of ambition or necessity, can create a condition for brokenness.

A tremendous impact is made on the mind of a child who daily observes dysfunctional parents. Many people who know they struggle with issues from their past don't report disturbing childhood incidents, but simply recognize that their parents suffered from low self-esteem. It is often enough to witness a parent cope daily with the debilitating weight of low self-worth to create similar emotional struggles in a child.

The heart of a child can experience brokenness in numerous ways. Often it's not just one particular incident, but a series of events, a pattern of behavior, or adverse living conditions that is the perpetrator of the real heart damage. Or all of the above!

Again, we aren't blaming parents or pointing fingers of accusation. Brokenness can occur in a child when parents are doing the best they can—as most parents are. Frequently it happens because the parents are broken too.

Parental authority provides spiritual and emotional protection, much like a covering or a hedge provides a barrier to keep predators away. As guardians of the hedge, parents ultimately have the sacred responsibility of maintaining the integrity of a shield of protection around their children at all times. (This authority can extend to grandparents and other authority figures, but it primarily belongs to the parent.)

It's impossible to exaggerate the importance of this protective boundary because, unfortunately, the hedge can be broken or breached—through abuse, neglect, or adverse childhood conditions, such as those mentioned. Sometimes parents are in such a broken condition themselves, they are incapable of maintaining their parental authority.

Moreover, children need protection from both parents, Mom and Dad. When either parent fails to maintain the protective hedge, willingly or otherwise, a fracture can develop, placing the child in a dangerous position.

Children without spiritual protection are ultimately vulnerable to enemy advances. When the heart of a child is compromised, the devil will take advantage if he can. He will step through the fractured hedge with his chains of shame and hopelessness. Once that happens, a new heart bondage is created.

Chains on the Heart

We must acknowledge not only the crippling influence of chains on the heart, but also their actual spiritual presence. If we could see into the spirit world, we would see angels, demonic creatures, and other features not visible to the natural eye. We would be able to recognize chains of bondage on people.

Picture a person with an iron band around their midsection. Attached to the band is a heavy chain. The burden of the chains is not enough to kill the individual, but it is heavy enough to prevent freedom of movement. This illustration demonstrates how the enemy places bonds of shame and hopelessness on a damaged heart: *with spiritual chains*. These bonds or chains of shame implement the damage that is perpetrated by a heart bondage.

Deliverance is a recurrent theme in the Bible, from Genesis to Revelation. Jesus said He came to release those who are bound.

> "The Spirit of the Lord is upon me, because he has anointed me to proclaim good news to the poor. He has sent me to proclaim liberty to the captives and recovering of sight to the blind, to set at liberty those who are oppressed, to proclaim the year of the Lord's favor."
> —Luke 4:18–19

> **Broken children grow up to be broken adults, ashamed of who they are.**

"To proclaim liberty to the captives . . . "

One who is chained is a captive. We will call this a *broken person*. It's essential to recognize that broken people can still live productive lives just as whole people do. An emotional injury does not ruin a person or render them unfit for life. Absolutely not! However, life is more difficult for those who are bound. Broken children grow up to be broken adults, ashamed of who they are.

GUILT: Feeling bad because of something you have done.
SHAME: Feeling bad because of who you are.

Note the emphasis on the difference between guilt and shame. These two words often travel together in sentences: "He hung his head in guilt and shame."

If you have hurt someone or done something wrong, or even if you think you might have, you could feel guilty. That is quite normal and can also be healthy. Guilt is not necessarily bad, because it suggests you're taking moral responsibility for your actions. Feeling guilty is usually related to remorse, and it's always *associated with behavior,* including acts not yet committed. The actual offense can be real or imagined. Perhaps you feel bad because of something you have done or thought about doing or neglected to do. Or maybe you feel bad for being more fortunate than someone else. Either way, guilt is a feeling related to your behavior.

Shame is an entirely different matter. Shame can be a painful feeling arising from your behavior or the behavior of those associated with you. Still, shame is more related to *who you are* because of that behavior. Shame is about identity, and it's strongly associated with disgrace. It's a terrible thing to be ashamed of who you are.

Altered Identity

I will never forget my reaction to the words that changed the course of my life. Just eight years old, I was completely unaware of and unprepared for the harshness of the new reality I was about to face.

"Other people don't think we're as good as they are."

"You can play with the other children, but they'll never accept you."

A mere handful of words spoken in the span of a few seconds struck hard and deep, breaking my heart and impressing a deep sadness. Those words had a strange power. They were spoken by one who had the authority that only a parent can hold over a child. Somehow I was able to grasp the implications of what had happened. How incredible that a little girl of eight years could comprehend the power of the spoken word and the spiritual authority of a parent!

After that day, I changed. I became somewhat withdrawn, and I often felt isolated and alone. I thought I was on my own in the world, sure that I could trust no one, and unable to relate well to my classmates at school. I was aware of my musical and creative talents, but that didn't seem to help me any, because all my gifts seemed to add up to nothing. Though I couldn't explain why, I didn't believe anyone else would ever recognize my value. I felt invisible and undeserving, as though I didn't count and didn't belong. Against all reason, I knew *I was a nothing and a nobody, and I didn't matter.* Silently I grieved as I wrestled with the most dreadful certainty that nothing I did would ever matter. And that could never be changed. *Ever.*

Eight years old, and I had no hope. I was broken.

During my teen years, I was desperate to grow up and start my own life. I knew I had serious problems with my self-worth. Still I thought that might improve if I could remove myself from the negative influences of home and look for opportunities to develop a career.

The challenges I faced at home were multifaceted. My father was sick much of the time, permanently disabled when I was fifteen. We were poor, but I didn't consider that the worst thing. Besides, I wasn't planning on staying poor all my life. The curse of poverty never got into my soul, so I never saw myself as poor, but as one who was temporarily less fortunate. *I can make money later on*, I thought, and I kept my economic status in perspective.

I always had a strained relationship with my mother. We were what one might call *polar opposites*. While she was naturally efficient and neat, I was a creative child who was, in her words, "the biggest mess-maker I've ever seen." Like many complicated relationships, ours was not about who was right and who was wrong, but the inevitable clash of two people who were never on the same page.

My mother was from a strict ministry family. Her overtly religious lifestyle greatly enhanced her controlling tendencies. She enforced religious rules over me with a vengeance—but not over my siblings. I deeply respected my family's heritage, but I could not abide by the rules (and still can't). She always demanded more from me than she did her other kids, and her demands were never subtle. As a teenager, I resented the difference she made between her children. I was the trophy child, and I felt such pressure to be perfect.

My mother was diagnosed as clinically bipolar when I was eleven. At that time, she was hospitalized for several weeks. When she came home, she cried for what seemed to be several more weeks. In the aftermath of that breakdown, Mom suffered from a debilitating depression, which lasted the entire span of my childhood and beyond. Her depression was the source of much tension in our family. There was virtually no filter in our home environment to protect my siblings and me from witnessing the ravages of mental illness. We had front-row seats.

The disturbing aspect of living with a person with a bipolar disorder is the uncertainty. Every day is like a roll of the dice. You never know which person you're going to be dealing with from one day to the next—the happy person or the depressed one. I knew I couldn't blame my mother for her illness, but I couldn't depend on her either.

The walls I built around my heart kept going up. I was instinctively trying to protect myself, but at the same time, I had no idea I was doing it. The barriers helped me withstand the hardship, but they also turned me into one of the most defensive creatures who ever walked planet Earth.

I knew if I were ever to make a better life for myself, I had to search elsewhere. My hometown was a tiny rural community of approximately 1,200 people (and one stoplight), which offered limited opportunities for education, career, and cultural development. So after graduating from high school, I went away to college. My spirits were high as I eagerly entered this new phase of my life, fully expecting to leave my damaged self-worth behind.

The first few weeks were exciting as I met new friends and became familiar with college life. The routine was brisk and challenging, and I settled into it quickly. However, I was soon dismayed to find my own troubled self-assessment unchanged. Whatever it was that plagued me back home had followed me, and it didn't have anything to do with my geographic location.

I was alarmed. I had carried the weight of hopelessness for such a long time, and I was ready to get over it. Even in my hopeless condition, I had dared to think that if I could escape the negativity, the heaviness might go away, or at least diminish somewhat. But it had not gone away. And evidently it had not diminished because, for some strange reason, I had trouble looking people in the eye. I lived in fear that others would find out about me, or about who I wasn't. I was afraid everyone would discover I was a nothing and a nobody, and that I didn't matter.

I knew I must confront myself about these feelings. Something was going on, and I was determined to get to the bottom of it. I felt a powerful urge to find an answer, and I felt almost led by a force beyond myself to try something I'd never done before. I decided to have a serious talk with myself, to do some real soul-searching. So one afternoon, I went to my dorm room when I knew I would be alone. I was a bit apprehensive, but I refused to be afraid. I wanted to know what was wrong. I wasted no time. I turned out the light and sat down on the bed with my back against the wall. Closing my eyes, I quieted my thoughts and, in total silence, began to look within. I was not prepared for what I was about to see.

Suddenly my eyes opened in my torso region. Though my eyes were closed, I could see inside my body as clearly as with my natural vision. I saw my inner person, which I recognized as my soul. The surface of my inner person was smooth and looked a lot like a muscle, and it took up almost all of my internal cavity. But there was something else too—a thick iron band and a heavy chain. The band wrapped around my inner person, my soul, in the middle like a belt. It wasn't too tight or too loose;

it fit perfectly. The band appeared continuous with no lock or joint or seam to indicate how it was attached. I had the impression it had been welded on.

Connected to the band was the chain, the length of it trailing off into the gloom. I couldn't see the end of it. The entire mechanism appeared clean and without rust nor marred by overuse. I saw no blood or gore. As I viewed my inner person and the strange device, I felt no fear. I remained calm and unemotional the whole time.

My inner vision seemed to last only a moment. Suddenly, as quickly as I had entered the vision, I felt pulled back. Once out, I opened my eyes and the shock of what I had seen threatened to overwhelm me. I had been looking for answers that afternoon, but this was more than I'd expected to find in my wildest imaginations. I had no idea what I'd seen, but it was something in me. The thought was now terrifying.

Near panic, I walked the hallway outside my dorm room, trying to calm myself. I knew I was dealing with something way out of my scope of experience or understanding. The device appeared to be permanent, which made it even more terrifying. The word *welded* came to me again and again, reinforcing the impression that the iron band could not come off. I didn't know what to do about it. I longed for some guidance, someone to talk to—*but who?* Who would believe me when I told them I'd seen my soul—with chains and an iron band attached to boot! (*Sure, sweetheart, you come with us; we'll take you where you won't see any more chains . . .*)

I didn't know what the device was, but I was sure it was the cause of the heaviness and shame I'd felt most of my life. It was *in me*, as though a part of me. I recognized it as a spiritual presence, not a physical one, although that made it no less real. I thought it must be a result of some kind of damage. But I knew it was not supposed to be there. I hated the intrusion. It appeared to be just what it felt like: *a ball and chain*.

I finally calmed myself by reasoning that the iron band with the chain was nothing new. Though I'd just had my first view of it, I'd felt its presence for many years. It had been there for a very long time. Realizing that, I considered I was not in any immediate danger, at least no more than before I discovered it.

That day in my dorm room, at eighteen years of age, I encountered a mountain. Convinced that this thing on my life—and the resulting heaviness—was not going to go away, I could only guess at its purpose. Although I didn't know what the device was, I did have enough insight to understand that it had something to do with my past and my family. Something from my childhood. Now looking back, I can see clearly. I was face to face with a *generational curse*.

CHAPTER TWO WORKBOOK

IT'S ALL ABOUT THE HEART

1. This study is about the condition of *the heart*. TRUE/FALSE

2. Write out Proverbs 4:23:

3. "Dealing with issues from childhood doesn't require that you disrespect your family."

   Do you think you can talk about your childhood honestly without disrespecting or dishonoring anyone? How?

4. This study is not about your parents, your grandparents, your relatives, or any other authority figures from your past. It's about _____.

5. "Often, a negative impact is made on the mind of a child through seemingly ordinary situations that are less than traumatic."

   Name three adverse childhood situations or conditions that are "less than traumatic" that could initiate a heart bondage. Circle any you experienced personally.

   1. _____
   2. _____
   3. _____

6. Parental authority provides spiritual and emotional protection, much like a covering or _____ provides a barrier or boundary to keep predators away.

7. Do you believe you have a heart bondage? Explain.

8. Describe what happened in your childhood to shape your life in a negative way. (Note: There may be more than one answer.)

9. The enemy places bonds of shame and hopelessness on a damaged heart with:

   a. depression
   b. thoughts of suicide
   c. overwhelming guilt
   d. spiritual chains

10. In Luke 4:18–19, Jesus named FIVE THINGS He came to do. List them:

    1. _____
    2. _____
    3. _____
    4. _____
    5. _____

11. What is the difference between GUILT and SHAME?

12. Shame is about your IDENTITY, and it's strongly associated with _____.

🔥 🔥 🔥

BONUS QUESTION: The heart bondage is more commonly found in:

   a. girls
   b. boys
   c. both—brokenness occurs in both genders equally.

CHAPTER THREE

Understanding Spiritual Bondage

Now that we know how chains are bound to the heart, what shall we call that device? Throughout this book, I most often refer to it as a *heart bondage*. I may also call it a *heart issue* or simply a *bondage*. I sometimes refer to *chains on the heart*, *emotional injury*, or I might call it a *generational curse*. The Bible uses the term *stronghold* (2 Corinthians 10:4). Surely, it is all these things. And it is most certainly the *bondage of shame*.

A heart bondage has five qualifying characteristics.

1) A heart bondage is made of lies.

There is no truth in a heart bondage. Chains on the heart are made up entirely of lies. That does not mean, however, that a heart bondage is not real. It is very real, and it has very real consequences.

The enemy, Satan, can deal only in lies because the truth is not in him. He can operate only in darkness because no light is in him. All his tools, his means, his very essence, are lies—lies and darkness.

> *For the weapons of our warfare are not carnal but mighty in God for pulling down strongholds . . .*
> —2 Corinthians 10:4 (NKJV)

In this verse, the Apostle Paul openly refers to warfare. If there is a war, we must be fighting against something that could hurt us. Otherwise, there'd be no need to fight. So although the devil operates only with lies and darkness, those lies have great potential to do harm to the children of God. In this scripture, that threat is called a *stronghold*.

> **Chains on the heart are made up entirely of lies. That does not mean, however, that a heart bondage is not real. It is very real, and it has very real consequences.**

Strongholds are tools of the enemy that are *strong*, and they seek to get a firm *hold* in your mind. *Strongholds*. A heart bondage is one type of stronghold.

This tool of the enemy, which we call a *heart bondage*, is a spiritual weapon of the kingdom of darkness. The weapon is built of lies, initiated for the express purpose of doing harm.

Your low self-esteem is a lie.

Your shame is a lie.

Your self-blame is a lie.

Your fear is a lie.

Your confusion is a lie.

Your hopelessness is a lie.

Knowing that low self-worth is a lie, however, is not enough to resolve self-worth issues. Those with a heart bondage are often aware of their strengths, capabilities, and gifts. Yet the lies of self-blame, shame, and hopelessness overshadow all good reason. Bound people know the truth about themselves, but the truth—the good they know—is rendered powerless by the lies and untruths. Lies attempt to usurp the place of truth.

Here is an excerpt from my testimony:

> *"I remember thinking I didn't believe what she said was true but somehow it became true, because she was my mother, and she believed it. For some reason I didn't understand, she had the authority*

to make it true because she had spoken it over me. It became as she had said."

The lie usurped the truth. The devil managed to twist things to his advantage by using the misguided authority of a parent as a loophole to claim that which was never lawfully his. "Usurp" means *to seize and hold without legal right*.

The devil has no right whatsoever to claim a position in your life, to maintain any authority over you, or to impose his will upon yours. He knows that. So he has to lie, cheat, and steal in the effort to make those gains. He simply cannot accomplish his objectives in any other way.

Satan moves in darkness because lies cannot thrive in the light. The lies of a heart bondage work closely with fear and confusion which, all together, are incredibly convincing and easily confused with the truth.

2) A heart bondage administers shame and hopelessness.

The hallmark of a heart bondage is *low self-esteem*. Most people with a heart bondage are aware that they struggle with a low sense of self-worth. Interestingly though, some do not recognize it as such. Those who don't, however, will experience it in other ways. It's a fact that some people are more in tune with their inner person than others.

Shame is about who you are. Shame is about identity, not behavior. Any conscientious person might be ashamed or embarrassed when they think of times they've misbehaved, but that's not what we're talking about here. The shame of a heart bondage *has nothing whatsoever to do with what you did*. It's more about the behavior of others, especially the authority figures in your life, and how that reflects on you. Shame accuses because of *what has been done to you, what you have experienced, or what you have witnessed*.

Hopelessness uses shame as a springboard. Hopelessness delivers the condemning message that nothing you do will ever matter because there is *no way out*. You're trapped.

When you have no hope, it's not so much that you have a problem—you believe *you are part of the problem*. And that's the real nail in the coffin with hopelessness. When you're convinced that your struggles are attached to you because of who you are, because of your flawed identity, or because of your inability to get it right or an innate weakness, then you'll believe the fault lies with you. You'll be convinced in your heart of hearts that you are a flawed creature, and—just as I did—start thinking that you're outside the scope of divine help. Hopelessness even goes so far as to suggest that God is against you too, because you are a part of the problem. That kind of thinking creates a cycle of despair.

I remember thinking God could not help me. Although I've always believed in God's supernatural power, I felt my brokenness was outside the realm of God's hand. I thought my emotional issues were founded on some kind of fault in my inner person, something God could not fix. My thoughts were, "Yes, God can do miracles, but He cannot change who I am."

That's hopelessness. Hopelessness is a progenitor to desperation. Desperate times call for desperate measures, right? Well, the desperate measures of hopelessness usually equate with poor decisions made with the detrimental influence of a heart bondage. It's incredible how hopelessness and shame can twist the reasoning and confound the common sense of the sanest of people.

> **The Lord will help anyone who calls on His name, even those who've been their own worst enemy.**

Perhaps you've made some serious mistakes in your life, decisions you deeply regret. You may have difficulty moving on because you believe you don't deserve it. Maybe you think you're in so deep you'll never get out. Whether or not you feel you're personally responsible for the condition of your life, that is not an issue with God.

Let's talk about that—who God is willing to help. Will the Lord only help the oppressed, those who are victims of injustice and hardship? Or will He help those who've consistently made terrible choices—those who, with their eyes wide open, dug a pit for themselves (and then jumped in)? The answer is *yes*. The Lord will help anyone who calls on His name, even those who've been their own worst enemy. He will help you as long as you're willing to take responsibility and accept change. He can show you how you got where you are and, more importantly, how to move beyond where you are. God doesn't have to delete your past to open new doors and create a new path for your future.

If you're convinced there is no way out and you'll never be happy, healthy, free, or even normal, you are experiencing *hopelessness*. This ugly beast is a twin sister to the ugly beast called shame, and they work in concert to create a grand deception. These are the products of the lies that constitute a heart bondage.

3) A heart bondage is about your identity.

I often address the influence that shame has upon *identity*. The primary purpose of a heart bondage is to attack your identity, plain and simple. However, you should know that your true identity is not in peril. It never was.

Your true identity is who God says you are. It's who God created you to be. That has never changed, nor will it ever change, because it's what God decreed when He designed and created you. His Word is unchangeable and irrefutable.

A heart bondage cannot change your real identity, but it seeks to alter your *perception* of who you are. This challenge to your understanding is a contradiction to what the Word of God says. It's an argument with the Word.

> *... casting down arguments and every high thing that exalts itself against the knowledge of God ...*
> —2 Corinthians 10:5 (NKJV)

Within the mind of a bound person is an ongoing conflict, a constant dispute about their identity. This dispute is much like a war or a battle against all good reason—indeed an argument that makes no sense whatsoever. Yet it continues. On and on, every day it continues to blame and slander. Even the brightest, most talented people wrestle

EMOTIONAL BONDAGE

Emotional bondage is generally understood as the inability to manage feelings or emotions. A sense of low self-worth is usually present, accompanied by deeply embedded negative thought patterns and substantial emotional pain. Self-contempt is common, as is the feeling of dragging a weight, or "baggage." Those with emotional bondage often feel isolated, unworthy, and ill-equipped to meet the pressures of life. In The Freedom Class, we recognize these negative vibes as the symptoms of an identity crisis which is the driving force behind dysfunction.

EMOTIONAL FREEDOM

Emotional freedom is associated with a positive self-image, the ability to manage emotions, and sound psychological health. Those who possess emotional intelligence learn to experience happiness, increase their capacity to love, set healthy boundaries, and focus on the positives. Emotional freedom liberates one from fear and insecurity, and shifts the focus from seeking acceptance to self-acceptance. In The Freedom Class, we understand that emotional freedom is attained by connecting with our God-ordained identity, who God says we are, and we refuse to be defined by rejection or the opinions of others.

consistently with demeaning accusations of unworthiness despite their abilities.

This argument is always about *you*. It's about *who you are*.

Anyone can see with the eyes of reason, logic, and common sense that we are all unique and valuable. Even without considering our individual gifts and talents, we are valuable simply because we are created by God and made in His image. Still, in the mind of the bound person, a silent inner voice refutes that knowledge. Negative thoughts continually condemn them for being who they are, and it accuses them so they feel bad about themselves. (That's *shame*.) A heart bondage will defy and challenge one's identity, regardless of all the accomplishments they may stack up. It's confusing, yes, but the bound person cannot get around it. They cannot push past it, and it never goes away. A bound person will always struggle with the fear, uncertainty, and confusion founded in an identity crisis.

The concept of *identity* is enormous. It's the first thing the enemy comes after, so obviously identity is a big deal with the devil. Satan even dared to confront Jesus Christ about who He was.

Just as Jesus was about to begin His ministry on earth, He fasted for forty days in the wilderness. At the end of that time, the devil came to Jesus to tempt Him to sin. The very first thing Satan challenged was Jesus's identity as the Son of God. He said, "If You are the Son of God, command this stone to become bread." —Luke 4:3.

"If You are the Son of God . . . "

Seeing that the devil challenged the identity of Jesus, does it strike you as strange that he might challenge yours? The devil knows *exactly* who you are. He just doesn't want you to know. Satan doesn't want you to realize your true identity because once you do, you'll recognize the power and authority you have in Christ. When that happens, the devil will have a fight on his hands that he knows he cannot win.

There is tremendous power in knowing who we are. Unfortunately, not enough believers comprehend their real identity, nor do they understand how the enemy uses deception to keep them from ever finding out. The Apostle Paul spoke numerous times of the believer's position "in Christ." Yet many Christians seem to think that has something to do with being super-spiritual, a label they apply only to a portion of life, like the religious part. As though they are "in Christ" on Sunday, but when they go to work on Monday morning, they're back to being just a regular person again. But actually, the "in Christ" status has a lot to do with the abundant life Jesus spoke of, and it's relevant to everyday life.

A heart bondage is an attack on our identity. Through shame, it seeks to convince us that we're someone other than who God says we are. A heart bondage always operates through the avenue of a distorted sense of low self-worth.

It's all about who you are.

4) A heart bondage is a consequence of rejection.

You have a divine right to be you. When God created you, He granted you a unique personality with a specific set of gifts and talents, and He assigned to you a purpose designated by Himself. All these characteristics sum up the very essence of who you are. You are distinct, a genuine individual. There never has been and never will be another person just like you. The divine right to be your authentic self is called your *personal authority*.

Rejection is one person's refusal to accept the personal authority of another. In the case of a heart bondage, the parent (or authority figure) refuses to recognize the child's personal authority and imposes their own interpretation onto the child. Rejection loudly proclaims, "This is who I say you are."

One young woman recounted how she suffered rejection from her father. When she was small, her dad refused to pay her any special attention or coddle her or tell her she was smart or pretty, things little girls need from a dad. For a long time, she tried to get his attention, but he was cold-hearted toward her. Try as she might, she failed to win his love or approval. Finally she gave up. Strangely, as an adult, she found herself unable to maintain a romantic relationship. The girl wondered what was wrong with her. She did everything she could to make herself lovable. She was beautiful, smart, and fabulously fit, but each of her romances failed one after the other.

One day in her thirties, she realized that she was silently communicating to men, *I'm not worthy of attention*. This young woman had a

> *There never has been and never will be another person just like you. The divine right to be your authentic self is called your personal authority.*

heart bondage associated with a specific brand of rejection. Because she considered herself unworthy of her father's love, she could not consider herself worthy of the love of any other man.

This true (and common) story is a classic example of the redefining power of rejection. Even if this little girl's father didn't realize what he was doing, he'd made a bold statement: "You aren't who you think you are. You think you're a little princess, but you're nobody special. You think you're smart and pretty, but I won't acknowledge it. You think you're lovable, but I won't validate that." The little girl believed what he said in his silence and lack of attention. When she grew up, that rejection manifested itself in her low self-worth and through her relationships.

Rejection begins with another's insecurities, and it's a form of sheer control. In this story, the girl's father was acting out of his own insecurities, even if in some morbid way we can't understand. (He probably didn't understand it either.)

In my own story, my mother was expressing her insecurities when she spoke words that shattered my confidence and redefined my self-image. Her insecurities didn't have anything to do with me. They had everything to do with her.

Every atrocity attributed to the breaking of a child can be traced to brokenness in the adult. Verbal abuse is the voice of damaged self-worth, just as excessive criticism is an act of fear. When a parent or other authority figure actively rejects a child, they are responding to old emotional injuries by expressing their fears and insecurities and passing them on to the next generation.

Attempting to define the "who" of another is nothing if not control. No one has the right to dictate identity except God, who created each human being a free moral agent. Who they are is God's business. But when parents abuse or neglect a child, that redefining force of rejection makes an indelible mark: "This is who I say you are." Parents who misuse their God-given authority in this way are actually transferring their own fears and insecurities onto the child. That's why it's called a *generational curse*.

Acts of rejection frequently occur through abuse, neglect, or adverse childhood conditions. When a parent or other authority figure makes the implicit declaration, "This is who I say you are," the child *believes it*. The child believes it because it's a statement made by someone who matters. Who in the life of a child is more significant than Mom or Dad? In the pain of rejection, the child is utterly convinced. A new self-image emerges in the child—not one that agrees with who God says they are, but one that accedes to who rejection says they are. And because parents strongly influence a child's view of God, the child now has a new image of God as well: *an image forged through the pain of rejection*.

An act of rejection by a parent or authority figure draws the child into the action and *poses them as part of the problem*. Even when the child knows they are innocent of wrongdoing, they will assume responsibility. This may not appear logical, but the heart is not always rational. As the seat of all emotion, the heart is highly sensitive to matters of trust and confidence. When a parent violates a child's faith, the child's heart will reflect that compromise, much like a cracked foundation. The child will assume responsibility for the abuse because rejection demands that they do so. It's who they are. They don't have to understand it, but they know it. They cannot escape it. An unlawful act has redefined the child's sense of identity, and they are ashamed.

> "When God created you, He automatically gave you not only power but permission to act out your authority; He gave you permission to be yourself." —Myles Munroe, *The Purpose and Power of Authority*[1]

---

1. Myles Munroe. *The Purpose and Power of Authority: Discover the Power of Your Personal Domain*, Whitaker House, 2010. 128.

5) A heart bondage produces accusation.

Accusation is a large part of a heart bondage, and it keeps the bound person silent. A broken child will rarely cry for help because they are ashamed. They feel the need to protect themselves by hiding their secrets because, in their heart of hearts, *they believe they are the problem.*

Shame is the ultimate silent weapon. The devil wants to keep everything in darkness as much as possible. He knows that a child silenced by shame usually won't cry out for help and won't take it to God either—even as an adult—because of their self-perceived involvement. Their thinking is, *How can I take this to God? He will punish me!* The broken person believes they have to hide what happened, and they have to hide who they are. In their mind, *what happened* and *who I am* are the same.

Remaining silent is the worst thing a broken person can do. But it's just what the enemy wants because his tools of despair only work in darkness. They do not work in the light. Shame seeks to isolate a person through silence, and in so doing, strengthens and protects the heart bondage. The enemy wins when broken people remain silent.

Silence driven by shame and accusation will usually cause the broken person to withdraw into themselves to some degree. This is called *isolation*. Through isolation, broken people often feel unable to dive into the mainstream of life, as though they don't belong. They may suspect they're different from everyone else, alone in their affliction. They may sincerely believe they're the only person in the world who suffers from such detachment.

Isolation is a self-imposed disconnect created solely for the purpose of self-protection. When a person feels isolated, it's proof-positive that those defensive walls are present—barriers intended to keep out the bad stuff and help the bound person endure hardship and pain. But the walls keep out the good stuff too, often resulting in defensiveness and emotional detachment. Broken people rarely trust anyone.

This is what I said in my testimony:

> "*Immediately I began building up walls around my heart. I didn't realize I was building anything like walls, but I surely was; and within a short time, those internal defenses were impenetrable. My*

³ For though we walk in the flesh, we do not war according to the flesh.

⁴ For the weapons of our warfare are not carnal but mighty in God for pulling down strongholds,

⁵ casting down arguments and every high thing that exalts itself against the knowledge of God, bringing every thought into captivity to the obedience of Christ . . .

2 Corinthians 10:3–5 (NKJV)

self-worth was severely damaged. Outwardly I could appear bright and outgoing; but on the inside, those walls were a steel fortress. They protected that shameful place from exposure and created a barrier to keep others out. Without a doubt, I knew I was a nothing and a nobody, and I didn't matter."

The weight of shame is entirely founded on one's identity and reinforced through accusation. Logically I was not responsible for my shame. I hadn't done anything to deserve such a weight on my life. Yet I believed I was responsible because the accusations were attached to my identity. I thought it was up to me to change my identity, but I couldn't. I tried to live my life in such a way that I could overcome and step out of the shadows, but I couldn't do that either. I spent decades trying to outrun the accusations and self-blame, to no avail. It was in me, part of me, and I was utterly helpless in the face of it. There was no way out. That is *shame and hopelessness*.

Through accusation, shame condemns us because of who we are. A heart bondage demands that we bear the responsibility for these wicked accusations, even though it doesn't make sense. It doesn't have to make sense, as long as we know we are part of what's wrong. That's the devil's game. That is *accusation*.

CHAPTER THREE WORKBOOK

UNDERSTANDING SPIRITUAL BONDAGE

1. Chains on the heart are made up entirely of _____. That does not mean, however, that a heart bondage is not real. It is very real, and it has very real _____.

2. Write out 2 Corinthians 10:4–5:

3. Shame is about your _____, not your _____.

4. Describe HOPELESSNESS.

   Have you experienced hopelessness in your life? YES/NO

   If so, explain.

5. "The desperate measures of hopelessness usually equate with poor decisions made with the detrimental influence of a heart bondage."

   What poor decisions have you made because of emotional injury?

6. The primary purpose of a heart bondage is to attack:

   a. your finances
   b. your relationships
   c. your health
   d. your identity

7. "Within the mind of a bound person is an ongoing conflict, a constant dispute about their identity."

   Have you experienced that *inner conflict* which is a CONSTANT ARGUMENT about your identity? If so, how?

8. Why does the devil want to keep you from knowing who you are?

9. REJECTION is one person's refusal to accept the personal authority of another. TRUE/FALSE

10. What is PERSONAL AUTHORITY?

    List five things associated with your own personal authority: (Ex: something about your personality, your talents, your position in your family, etc.) Note: These are things God says about you or assigned to you.

    1. _____
    2. _____
    3. _____
    4. _____
    5. _____

11. Debbie says that when parents abuse or neglect a child, they are transferring their own fears and insecurities onto the child.

    Have you seen this in your own life? If so, how?

12. Describe ISOLATION.

    Have you experienced isolation? Explain.

🔥 🔥 🔥

BONUS QUESTION: Only ONE PERSON has the right to dictate identity. Who?

CHAPTER FOUR

How a Heart Bondage Works

ALL HEART BONDAGES WORK THE SAME WAY. IN DEscribing the functions of a heart bondage, I use the word *abuse* frequently. But as you've already seen, the catalyst for emotional injury doesn't doesn't always have to classify as actual abuse. Other events—such as neglect, adverse childhood conditions, or merely the insecurity of well-meaning parents—can also play a dominant role in initiating a heart bondage. I use the word *abuse* here for the sake of brevity.

1) A heart bondage is applied at the time of abuse and is imprinted with exact instructions.

A heart bondage is positioned at the time of brokenness—not later when its effects appear. A heart bondage is attached when a child experiences abuse or neglect, and the protective hedge is no longer secure.

Because the chains go on at the time of a specific event, the bondage will resemble the activity that imposed it. You might picture it as shackles imprinted with *dictates,* instructions of a sort, that demand a continuation of that specific type of behavior or abuse. The dictates or instructions of a heart bondage create *patterns of behavior* that encourage a replication of the abusive action at a later time.

The behavior patterns of a heart bondage are implemented in the form of *thought processes*—simply a *way of thinking* embedded into the child's mind at the time of abuse. The thought patterns of a heart bondage result in defective and flawed mental habits, which will last a lifetime unless destroyed. They will eventually pass from the adult child to their children and then to their children. The duplication process is always for the next generation.

The broken thought processes inherited from one generation to the next will produce dysfunction in some form. Often there will be an exact repeat of the abuse: What the first generation did, the second will do also. The following true story is an excellent example of *exact duplication*.

Claudia was the oldest of eight children. Her family was poor, and her mother was sick most of the time. Even as a young girl, Claudia was responsible for much of the household chores and cooking. Claudia's domineering and overbearing grandmother ran the household, much to everyone's chagrin. Sadly, misogyny ran deep and wide in Claudia's family history. More than just a preference for the sons, an overt contempt for the girls prevailed. The grandmother often called Claudia and her sisters offensive names—smears associated with their femininity. These hateful names demeaned and belittled their value as young women. As an older woman, Claudia often spoke of her grandmother with a sense of awe and dread. She told how her grandmother had verbally and emotionally abused her and her sisters. Yet when she had granddaughters of her own, she was caught screaming the same obscenities at them.

Claudia demonstrated an exact duplication of abuse. Although she resented the insulting language directed at her as a child, she repeated it to the letter as an adult.

But the human heart is a complex thing, and response to abuse is not always that straightforward. While some will duplicate abuse exactly, as Claudia did, others will respond differently. Some will go the opposite way, much like a backlash or reverse reaction. In these cases, the ensuing dysfunction will not look quite the same as the original abuse, but nevertheless there is some relation between the two. My own story is an excellent example of a *reverse reaction to abuse*, which occurs when one is resistant to emotional injury and tries to outperform it.

In one way or another, the original abuse of a heart bondage will be replicated. The adult child duplicates the experience, witnessing either a recurrence of the abuse or a form of dysfunction stemming from that

> **Generational curses guarantee susceptibility to continuing dysfunction in families.**

abuse. It may take years for the imprint on the heart to reproduce itself, but it will happen.

This is how the enemy transports and duplicates a particular type of dysfunction from one generation to another. The majority of heart bondages are passed from one generation to the next; that's why they are called *generational "curses."* Generational curses guarantee susceptibility to continuing dysfunction in families. Many generational curses are transferred with words.

We can view a generational curse much as we would a genetic disease. If there is a cure available, but the patient refuses to take the treatment, the condition can pass to the next generation. Heart bondages are a lot like that. Someone needs to administer the cure to stop the curse from moving on to the next group of kids.

A specific kind of authority is needed to create the ideal conditions suitable for the implementation of a heart bondage. The type of authority that parents have over their children is the kind that works best. Heart bondages are not created by parents, however. A heart bondage is a tool of the enemy, implemented by forces of darkness. Parents do allow the ideal conditions for a heart bondage to occur. Still, I believe the vast majority of parents do this unaware.

2) A bound person will lose the ability to control their behavior in specific areas.

A bound person absolutely must act according to the dictates. As long as the heart bondage is attached, it is in control to some degree.

The dictates imprinted on a heart bondage are a lot like programming. They make an indelible mark on the mind, affecting the thought processes significantly. These dictates—much like coded instructions—demand a continuation of the abusive behavior that caused the heart bondage at its inception. As we've seen, that specific dysfunction, or brokenness, will be duplicated in the life of the bound person, either as an exact duplication or a related dysfunction. The dysfunction dictated by a heart bondage is perpetual and *cannot be resolved until it's broken*. This fact alone is probably the most perplexing trait of a heart bondage.

If two boys are abused verbally, they may both have a heart bondage. But because of variations in personality, the boys will most likely respond differently. For example, let's assume both boys were told that they're worthless and stupid. The first boy may respond by dropping out of school at an early age. Perhaps he'll get involved with drugs and fail to hold a job. He knows he is worthless and stupid.

The second boy might do that too, or he may take another route. The second boy may struggle to prove himself by attaining the best education and developing a lucrative career. But regardless of how successful the second boy becomes, he cannot outperform the heart bondage. The accusation continues, as does the argument about his identity. He works harder and harder, trying to defeat the charge (that he is worthless and stupid) through performance. So while he can choose how he responds to the accusations, he cannot control the fact that he must respond. He can manage his response, but he cannot win the argument.

In this example, neither of the boys can resolve their brokenness. They simply respond differently. The first boy succumbs to the dictates while the second responds in dysfunction. The second boy is the type that becomes a workaholic. His career might be considered a blazing success, but his relationships suffer because of his internal focus on his weakness. His marriages fail, his family life is nonexistent, and his children grow up feeling confused and rejected because Dad didn't have time for them. (Now they have heart bondages too.)

Like the two boys, every person with a heart bondage must respond to that brokenness in some way. Successful people often hide their brokenness behind achievement. Success is an effective coverup, at least until others get too close.

Not surprisingly, broken people almost always attract broken people. Stepping from one dysfunctional situation into a similar one is comforting because it's familiar. Dysfunction relates to dysfunction. An inclination to repeat the pattern of dysfunction is part of the self-perpetuating machinery that so accurately describes how a heart bondage works.

3) A heart bondage operates automatically.

A heart bondage is somewhat like a machine. Once established on a human heart, it continues working automatically by default. It would appear the enemy and his evil forces don't have to do a lot of maintenance work on a heart bondage—perhaps none. That may be why he seems to favor this device. A heart bondage is extremely effective with very little work on the enemy's behalf because *the bound person keeps it operating*.

A heart bondage is a controlling mechanism that feels entirely natural. The thought patterns imposed by a heart bondage communicate through the mind, appearing to be natural reactions to the stress and pressures of life. The accusations of a heart bondage sound and feel like the person's own thoughts, as though they are accusing themself. A heart bondage has all the appearance of being part of the bound person's natural mental makeup.

> *A heart bondage is a controlling mechanism that feels entirely natural.*

The formation of negative thought patterns (the habit of negative thinking) is, like all habits, universally attributed to *repetition*. We form natural habits by repeating an action until that behavior becomes automatic. Eventually, after enough repetition, the behavior becomes second nature, and we do it without conscious effort. (Think nail-biting.) But the repetitive action necessary to form a natural habit is not required to establish the mechanics of a heart bondage.

A heart bondage is not created through repetition. It is a spiritual device consisting of an iron band and chains on the heart, and it works efficiently from Day One. A heart bondage is automatically repetitious. The ensuing emotional distress strengthens the bondage, causing the heart bondage to become stronger through time.

A heart bondage is not subject to the natural laws that create and destroy regular habits. We can break natural habits by discontinuing an undesired behavior and replacing it with something else. But a heart bondage is not a mere habit. Although it may appear to be a simple matter of negative thinking, a heart bondage is a spiritual tool of wickedness imposed for destruction. We must dismantle a heart bondage through spiritual means.

The pattern of negative thinking imposed by a heart bondage is always directed at one's identity. It's an accusation, an argument concerning *who they are*. This argument originates from the heart—in the mind, where the bondage is located. It is projected through the thoughts, resulting in low self-worth, hopelessness, and confusion.

4) A heart bondage operates secretly.

A heart bondage operates with a great deal of stealth. Because it is a spiritual tool that feels completely natural, its presence is extremely subtle. Usually, a broken person cannot identify their struggle. They may acknowledge they have issues, but they're unable to locate the cause. There's no label they can pin to it, no real clarity, but perhaps a vague awareness that something is not right. Often they conclude that they simply have low self-esteem. Bound people feel the effects of their chains, but most do not even realize they are bound.

People cannot rid themselves of something they don't know they have. Like seeing a doctor for a physical ailment, a correct diagnosis is necessary before treatment can begin. Most bound people never get that diagnosis.

This incognizance is the reason most heart bondages are never torn down. The vast majority of bound people live and die with a heart bondage intact. It's easy to become so used to the oppression, it becomes the norm. When it has always been this way, it feels familiar. Most people assume it's just a part of life.

A heart bondage does not wear off, nor does the element of time alleviate its influence. A heart bondage has lifelong sticking power. It can become stronger as years pass because it operates automatically, and that process can strengthen the chains.

> **Understanding the heart bondage solves the riddle that has puzzled many people through struggle, confusion, heartbreak, and very often a string of bad decisions even they never entirely understood.**

When I share my story with a group, I can usually tell who among them has a heart bondage. For them, it's a grand slam. *They get it!* It's practically universal. By identifying with my story, broken people immediately recognize the presence of a heart bondage in themselves. The most common reaction I sense from them is *relief*—as if they've been hoping and waiting for a diagnosis.

Most people are not upset to discover that they have a heart bondage, nor do they try to deny it. They're just so glad to find out what it is! They're delighted to get some clarity about their perplexing emotional state. *Heart bondage* is a simple term for a common but complex identity crisis. Understanding the heart bondage solves the riddle that has puzzled many people through struggle, confusion, heartbreak, and very often a string of bad decisions even they never entirely understood.

But now the secret is exposed. Like a correct diagnosis, identifying a heart bondage brings enlightenment and hope. Your newfound knowledge about the heart bondage should explain a lot about your inner struggle. A heart bondage is a powerful and highly effective tool designed to accomplish destruction.

> "Virtually nothing we come up against in our individual Christian lives is more formidable than a stronghold . . . Strongholds are broken one way only: they have to be demolished."
> —Beth Moore[2]

---

2. Beth Moore. Praying God's Word: Breaking Free from Spiritual Strongholds. B & H Books, 2009. 5.

CHAPTER FOUR WORKBOOK

HOW A HEART BONDAGE WORKS

1. Every heart bondage works the same way. TRUE/FALSE

2. A heart bondage is applied:

    a. at the time of brokenness
    b. years after the abuse, when the effects of brokenness appear
    c. when the child grows up
    d. none of the above
    e. all of the above

3. What is the purpose of the DICTATES (or instructions) of a heart bondage?

4. The behavior patterns of a heart bondage are implemented in the form of THOUGHT PROCESSES—simply a _____ _____ _____.

5. Generational curses guarantee susceptibility to continuing dysfunction in:

    a. the community
    b. the church
    c. the family
    d. groups of friends

6. Do you see a generational curse in your own family? If so, describe it. (Note: Look for similar dysfunctional behavior among family members of different ages.)

7. "A bound person will lose the ability to control their behavior in specific areas."

Have you experienced this in your own life? If so, explain.

8. The dysfunction dictated by a heart bondage is perpetual and cannot be _____ until it's broken. This fact alone is probably the most perplexing trait of a heart bondage.

9. "Broken people almost always attract broken people."

   Have you witnessed this in your own life or in the lives of people you know? Explain.

10. Why does a heart bondage feel so natural, like your own thoughts?

11. "A heart bondage operates secretly."

    How does a heart bondage stay a secret?

12. Most people are not upset to discover that they have a heart bondage. TRUE/FALSE

🔥 🔥 🔥

BONUS QUESTION: What is your reaction to your new knowledge about the heart bondage? Explain.

CHAPTER FIVE

Serious Symptoms

A PERSON WITH A HEART BONDAGE WILL WITNESS A manifestation of that bondage in some way. The word "manifest" means *perceived by the eye*. When something manifests, you see it. Although a heart bondage is a spiritual tool, invisible to the natural eye, its effects will appear to be anything but spiritual. They are entirely visible and will show up in daily life in a variety of ways.

The thief comes only to steal and kill and destroy.
I came that they may have life and have it abundantly.
—John 10:10

In this verse, Jesus refers to Satan as a "thief" who has wicked intentions toward humanity. Because you're a child of God, you're in the line of fire. The devil wants to steal from you when he can, kill you if he can, and destroy you in any way he can.

Actual physical death is not necessary for the enemy to accomplish his purposes, however. If Satan can immobilize people so they never develop to their full potential, he can consider that a win. He seriously wants to ruin the special relationship people have with God. Humans are anointed or empowered by Heaven to accomplish God's will on the

> **Serious Symptoms are the manifestation, or result, of dysfunctional thought processes.**

Earth. A threat to him, for sure! So he does what he can to prevent people from living in the light and joy of spiritual and emotional freedom. The heart bondage is a tool he uses to accomplish that by getting people stuck in the mire of shame and hopelessness early in life.

While destruction is the enemy's intention, *self-imposed destruction* appears to be his preference. Through the use of a heart bondage, Satan attempts to get people to participate in their own demise. Shame and hopelessness lay the trap for desperation. With great deception and stealth, the enemy urges people into harmful behavior patterns which, over time, lock them into destructive lifestyle habits. These behavior patterns create emotional storms that can keep people in a cycle of fear and failure, sometimes for decades. I refer to the effects of a heart bondage as *Serious Symptoms*.

Serious Symptoms are the manifestation, or result, of dysfunctional thought processes. They act as a hindrance, often preventing people from being productive and going forward with their lives. Serious Symptoms introduce a greater susceptibility to traumatic events. The severity of the Symptoms ranges from mild to urgent, even life-threatening. They can become so critical they take center stage and sometimes cause people to neglect the basic necessities of life. Though Serious Symptoms are often an escape from the pain of a heart bondage and its characteristic identity crisis, they only add fuel to the fire. Serious Symptoms are painful in their own way and act as a catalyst for dysfunction.

The three big predictors of a heart bondage are shame, hopelessness, and low self-worth. Beyond that, other prevalent indications are confusion, fear, anxiety, and depression. (The depression of a heart bondage often appears as a general heaviness.) These facets of emotional turbulence result in significant despair and emotional pain. Varying levels of emotional pain always accompany a heart bondage.

A hurting person will often seek to escape the pain through whatever means is available. Research consistently reports that abused or neglected children are at a much higher risk of using alcohol and illicit drugs in adulthood.

A comprehensive report, The Adverse Childhood Experiences Study, states: "In fact, male children with an ACE Score of 6 or more (having six or more adverse childhood experiences) had an increased likelihood—of more than 4,000 percent—to use intravenous drugs later in life." (Felitti & Anda , 2009)[3] *Four thousand percent!*

Living with Serious Symptoms is the challenging part of having a heart bondage. The Symptoms have a way of taking control and can be very painful for both the bound person and those close to them. Symptoms cripple the bound person spiritually and socially and are a significant factor in the struggle with relationships.

Not all Serious Symptoms appear detrimental, however. Many times a person will express their insecurities through seemingly altruistic conduct. Overly anxious and people-pleasing tendencies, obsessive servanthood, and codependent traits can be signs of deep emotional scars, as can a willingness to be abused.

Self-sacrifice without boundaries is a common Symptom of a heart bondage, especially among women. Always willing to make the peace, these do-gooders are ready to put themselves out there like a doormat. They make great codependent partners, as they consistently focus on the happiness of someone else, often at their own expense. Codependent partners feel a loyalty to those who would abuse them. They are willing to enable others, especially a spouse or romantic partner, even when that person (who also has a heart bondage) displays narcissistic traits. The do-gooders will take the beating or the verbal lashing, or perhaps forfeit their own basic needs so their loved one can live lavishly. Their behavior is the definition of dysfunctional, yet they always manage to feel honorable about it. Unfailingly, the enablers develop a martyr mentality. It's a feeble attempt to feel good about themselves.

As we discuss the Serious Symptoms as *lifestyle conditions*, note the defining word *lifestyle*. There is a big difference between a *temporary bout*

---

3. Felitti & Anda. Child Welfare Information Gateway Online, 2009. https://www.coursehero.com/file/p6q9pnu/One-study-using-ACE-data-found-that-roughly-54-percent-of-cases-of-depression/ Available at: https://www.childwelfare.gov/pubs/factsheets/longterm consequences.cfm

Examples of Serious Symptoms, lifestyle conditions that reflect the presence of a heart bondage:

- low self-esteem (the hallmark)
- self-loathing or self-contempt
- confusion
- depression
- anger
- fear
- anxiety
- abusive behavior, cruelty toward others (people or animals)
- violence
- willingness to be abused (acting as a doormat for others)
- antisocial traits
- excessive bragging
- habitual and chronic lying
- pervading sadness
- eating disorders (anorexia, bulimia)
- personality disorders
- inability to regulate emotion (ex: uncontrolled anger, violence, or fear)
- alcoholism

- all drug addiction
- addiction to sex or pornography
- food addiction
- uncontrollable jealousy
- promiscuity
- harming oneself (cutting, etc.)
- people-pleasing
- overzealous servanthood
- self-sacrifice without boundaries
- sexual dysfunction or perversities
- suicidal tendencies
- verbal or emotional cruelty
- attachment issues or inability to connect in emotional intimacy
- persistent lack of confidence

*Note: This is a partial list of Serious Symptoms. The complete list of Serious Symptoms due to a heart bondage is unknown because it's unique to each person's response to brokenness.

and a *lifestyle condition*. Anyone can become angry at themselves or suffer from occasional anxiety. But broken people are often enslaved by these dysfunctional behavior patterns. It's not just a temporary matter for them. They usually feel unable to stop, even as they despise themselves for their weakness. Those who struggle with the most severe Serious Symptoms often know their behavior is detrimental, even dangerous. Self-contempt is common among broken people who suffer from habits that, over time, destroy all vestiges of joy and peace.

The Serious Symptoms of a heart bondage, however painful, are not the source of brokenness. They are the resulting manifestation of the heart bondage. Serious Symptoms exist *because the heart bondage was in place first*. Any confusion about this matter stems from the fact that these lifestyle conditions (Serious Symptoms) are visible to the natural eye, while the heart bondage itself is not. Serious Symptoms appear to be the more urgent matter, and indeed they often are.

We can view a heart bondage and its Serious Symptoms by using an analogy of physical illness. If a person has the flu, they will have symptoms: fever, chills, sore throat, aches, pains. Their doctor should know what they have—the flu. He can treat the symptoms, and the patient might feel better. Still, the symptoms are apt to recur until the flu virus is gone. The fever and sore throat (the symptoms) provide the discomfort, but they are not the source of the illness; they are only the manifestation of the flu virus. You can see the symptoms, but the flu virus itself is invisible. The invisible virus is the real source of the sickness, the cause of all the symptoms. Once the flu virus disappears, the symptoms will disappear.

A bound person can get stuck in the Symptoms. Without a cure for the underlying cause, the conditions arising from a heart bondage can become urgent. They can consume the bulk of one's time, money, and efforts in the attempt just to survive, to manage the dysfunction. Those trapped in a cycle of despair rarely get around to pursuing the greater things in life, finding out who they really are, serving God and others, and generally enjoying life.

More About Serious Symptoms

A heart bondage consists partly of chains. Like any chain, it has links. The chains of shame contain within their links those things we recognize as Serious Symptoms—destructive mind-sets and habits, dysfunctional behavior patterns, chemical dependencies, addictions, etc. These links play a big part in how the heart bondage works.

The central part of the heart bondage (the iron band) is the only part directly attached to the person. It wraps around the heart and produces the brokenness. The chains, however, provide the weight. This is the heaviness that is so familiar to those with a heart bondage. All the chain links are connected, of course, giving rise to a continuous stream of dysfunction. Some links are "inherited" through the generational quality of the heart bondage, as certain dysfunctions tend to run in families.

The iron band draws energy from the bound person. It then passes that energy into the chains. That energy consists of pure fear, and it fuels the dysfunction and the destructive mind-sets that are housed there. So indirectly through the chains of shame, the conditions we recognize as Serious Symptoms derive all the strength and stamina they need from the brokenness of the heart bondage. They must have that brokenness to survive and thrive, to keep going, to perpetuate dysfunction.

But then an odd thing happens. The dysfunction and the destructive mind-sets of the chains, energized by the brokenness and fueled by fear, create a negative energy of their own: *confusion*. That confusion-energy is passed back into the iron band, fueling it for another round. This is the *vicious cycle* of fear and confusion that is so characteristic of brokenness and dysfunction.

The heart bondage is the energy supplier for all Serious Symptoms. It's where dysfunction draws its lifeblood, so to speak. But that "lifeblood" doesn't just materialize out of thin air; *it comes from the bound person*. The heart bondage interacts with the person in such a way that it converts the emotional distress of brokenness into the fear and confusion which stimulate and fuel the heart bondage. The bound person keeps it operating.

That's why the power of positive thinking is a sound doctrine to

> *Through reason, logic, and the application of practical wisdom, you can develop healthy attitudes and positive emotional responses that go a long way in waging the battle of the mind.*

some degree. Although managing your mind through attitude change won't eliminate a heart bondage, it can reign in the fear that drives dysfunction. Through reason, logic, and the application of practical wisdom, you can develop healthy attitudes and positive emotional responses that go a long way in waging the battle of the mind. The power of positive thinking is an attribute with or without a heart bondage.

But notice that the Serious Symptoms are not attached directly to the person. Instead, the dysfunction resides in the chains. The chains are there to impose the Symptoms, but they don't actually touch the heart of the bound person. This is very good news!

This is good news because it provides a lasting solution to discouragement. Multitudes of people know what it's like to fight the same old battle over and over. Whether it's drugs, eating disorders, alcohol, self-loathing, personality disorders, or whatever, they can't seem to get free of it or resolve it. They've tried various programs and therapy; they've been in and out of rehab clinics and quite possibly through a string of relationships. Yet they haven't been able to overcome that giant in their life, the one thing they can't seem to beat. Many are tempted to give up and quit, and unfortunately, some do.

But our knowledge of the heart bondage gives us hope. We can see that the Serious Symptoms, although painful, are dependent upon the presence of one particular entity to survive: *the heart bondage*. Once the heart bondage is broken, the band falls away along with the chains, and the landscape of life suddenly changes. Without the brokenness of the heart bondage from which to draw their energy, the Serious Symptoms weaken considerably. They lose their grip quickly when the mind is free from the shackles of shame and hopelessness. Once the battle for emotional freedom is won, the strength to overcome is powerfully present, and a glorious opportunity exists for the newly freed person to step over the chains and walk away.

It is typical of broken people to concentrate on treating the Serious Symptoms. That's understandable, and the right thing to do at times. An urgency accompanies real pain. It can be difficult to target the root of that pain when you're sidetracked by the real life situations associated with dysfunction. When you're in real pain, nothing else matters but to stop the hurting. At those times, it may seem almost impossible to see anything but the problem, the problem, the problem.

However, it's important to look beyond the immediate needs of the moment. If you look *beyond* the pain, you will see that the issues of childhood—*the heart bondage*—is at the core of your grief. Exhausting all your energy and efforts in managing the Serious Symptoms, however urgent, will deter you from curing the source. As long as the devil can keep you busy with the Symptoms, he can probably prevent you from ever doing anything about the heart bondage. And I can assure you the devil intends to keep you as busy as possible for as long as he can.

At the same time, Serious Symptoms do require attention. Like the symptoms of a natural illness, they can become dangerous, even life threatening. There is a time to seek help, a time for medical and professional intervention. If you need to get outside assistance, by all means do so now. But even as you treat the Serious Symptoms, do not neglect to address the heart issues. Until the source of the brokenness (the heart bondage) is resolved, you could be subject to fighting *a recurring battle*.

Denying the Victim Mentality

Before we continue, let's get one thing straight: In this study, *we will not play the victim*. And we aren't going to blame our problems on anyone else either. Although the presence of a heart bondage does promote negative thought patterns, every person is ultimately responsible for their own behavior. "The devil made me do it" doesn't apply here (or anywhere). *Your response to the pressures of life is your decision.*

A heart bondage has a tremendous influence on thought processes. However, that influence cannot force anyone to become addicted to drugs or alcohol, act out in anger, or harm someone else. The negative

> **Although the presence of a heart bondage does promote negative thought patterns, every person is ultimately responsible for their own behavior.**

mind-sets that accompany a heart bondage can only *encourage* dysfunction.

The circumstance of one's early life is a dominant factor in lifestyle. A child raised in a culture of violence will undoubtedly be more prone to committing violence. But then of course, we're back to how heart bondages are implemented—chains on the heart imprinted with *instructions*.

Let's flip our reasoning around for a moment and view this from another angle.

Those who exhibit Serious Symptoms almost always have a heart bondage. If you were to interview a group of people in an anger management class, you would find the vast majority of them, if not all, have a heart bondage. The prisons are full of men and women with multiple issues from childhood.

The choice to commit reprehensible deeds, however, is precisely that: *a choice*. There is no excuse for bad behavior. A heart bondage may present a tendency or a temptation to go a certain way. Still, no one has to respond to any temptation of any sort. Temptation is a suggestion, not a command. Depression, frustration, and anger are frequent battles with which bound people struggle, but acting out of those feelings is a matter of the will.

There is—*more good news!*—a viable solution to the threat of Serious Symptoms. The effects of the Serious Symptoms can be significantly reduced by living in obedience to the Word of God, which encourages the application of wisdom and a measure of self-discipline. God's Word commands a standard of righteousness, and those with a heart bondage are not exempt. Living in compliance with the principles of God's Word produces an abundance of benefits that will help you to develop your life in more positive ways.

CHAPTER FIVE WORKBOOK

SERIOUS SYMPTOMS

1. Write out John 10:10:

2. What are SERIOUS SYMPTOMS?

3. See the list of Serious Symptoms provided in this chapter. Have you sustained any of these lifestyle conditions or behavior patterns in your life, either now or in the past? If so, which ones? (Include any you have experienced that are not on the list provided.)

   Cross through those conditions that are no longer a problem for you.
   Underline the ones with which you still struggle.
   Place a check by the ones you are currently working on.
   Circle any that you thought were just a part of your personality.

4. The three big predictors of a heart bondage are shame, hopelessness, and:

   a. low self-worth
   b. drug-addiction
   c. codependent behavior
   d. sexual promiscuity
   e. none of the above

5. Many Serious Symptoms are obviously "bad" behavior. But some Serious Symptoms appear to be desirable personality traits. Name three below and circle any you've practiced:

   1. _____
   2. _____
   3. _____

6. "Self-sacrifice without boundaries is a common Symptom of a heart bondage."

   Does this sentence describe anyone you know? Who? Explain.

7. What is the difference between a *temporary bout* and a *lifestyle condition*?

8. What can happen when a person gets stuck in the Serious Symptoms?

   Has this ever happened to you? To someone you know? Describe what happened.

9. "The chains are there to impose the Symptoms, but they don't actually touch the heart of the bound person."

   Why is this good news?

10. Once the heart bondage is broken, and the band falls away, what happens to the chains?

    Does this give you hope? Why?

11. "Although the presence of a heart bondage does promote negative thought patterns, every person is ultimately responsible for their own behavior."

    Explain why we are NOT VICTIMS.

    Can you take responsibility for your own mistakes? YES/NO

12. The effects of the Serious Symptoms can be significantly reduced by living in obedience to:

    a. the law
    b. church rules
    c. what parents say
    d. the Word of God

BONUS QUESTION: Those who exhibit Serious Symptoms almost always have a heart bondage. TRUE/FALSE

CHAPTER SIX

Types of Strongholds

THE PRIMARY TARGET IN THIS STUDY IS *THE HEART BOND-age*. But often I am asked about other types of bondages and strongholds. Isn't alcoholism a bondage? Isn't drug addiction a bondage? What about eating disorders, isn't that a bondage?

The answer to these questions is an emphatic *yes*. We can correctly classify many different types of behavior patterns as *bondages* or *strongholds*. Some are created by an overindulgence of the flesh or pleasure-related pursuits. Others stem from an emotional state, such as unforgiveness, bitterness, or anxiety. And finally, some are *infirmities*, which is best described as a mental or emotional weakness.

These various behavior patterns are not heart bondages, but they are strongholds nonetheless. They are what I call *simple strongholds*. The term "simple" does not imply that these activities are harmless. But I use the word *simple* to categorize them as *strongholds that exist on their own*.

Many strongholds are created through repetition. The practice of consistently engaging a particular behavior can form attachments to that behavior, both emotionally and physically. Some examples are alcoholism, chemical dependency, chronic worry, gambling, smoking cigarettes—any behavior that becomes a habit through time and repetition. Most life-impacting habits are formed in adulthood or at least beyond the early years. Both good and bad habits are familiar to everyone. But once a bad habit gains a hold on the mind, it becomes a strong hostile force.

If a person insists on poor choices long enough, they can form their own personal array of custom-designed strongholds, created by none other than themself. All strongholds don't have to be from the devil.

Anyone can create a simple stronghold, even those who don't have a heart bondage. The habit of smoking cigarettes, for example, or pornography—an addiction that has risen to epidemic proportions in our nation. Although some pornography viewers (and smokers too) have heart bondages inevitably, many do not. The pleasure of illicit sensuality can entice both bound people and free.

You can see that there are many different types of bondages or strongholds. However, these simple strongholds are not the same as a heart bondage. So, what is the difference between a simple stronghold and a heart bondage? There are three significant distinctions.

1. Timing

    > A heart bondage is established during childhood.
    > A simple stronghold is established in adulthood or the teen years (usually).

2. Origin

    > A heart bondage is a device attached to the heart of a child at a time of abuse, neglect, or adverse childhood conditions. It is not initiated by the child. The child is not responsible.
    > A simple stronghold is a bondage created through unhealthy emotional states and repetitive behavior, or habit. It is initiated by the person with the bondage. The bound person is responsible.

3. Effects

    > A heart bondage imposes shame and hopelessness. It affects the thought processes and generally results in low self-worth, dysfunction, and confusion.
    > A simple stronghold is restricted to a single activity. (Ex: A gambling habit will result in a bondage to gambling.)

Heart Bondage

- Chains on the heart placed during childhood.
- Attached during abuse, neglect, or adverse lifestyle conditions.
- Imposes shame, hopelessness, and low self-worth, affecting thought processes.
- The bound person is not responsible for the heart bondage.

Simple Stronghold

- Destructive habits and mind-sets, usually developed in adulthood or the teen years.
- A result of choices and decisions, formed through repetitive behavior, or habit.
- Affects a specific behavior (gambling, alcoholism, or eating disorders, etc.).
- The bound person is responsible for the bondage, or habit.

Note: The above depictions of simple strongholds describe those acquired primarily through habit and do not apply to *infirmities*. An infirmity is a weakness, like a moral failure, something which one almost cannot help. Infirmities often appear early in life and are generally not acquired through repetition. Those with infirmities are not responsible for their condition. However, an infirmity is not a heart bondage. Although we may attribute the presence of an infirmity to a heart bondage, its effects impact a single activity or one area of behavior. It is a simple stronghold.

A heart bondage and simple strongholds *often exist together*. Anyone can form a bad habit, but a person with a heart bondage will almost always acquire a collection of lesser bondages. As a student of freedom, you will recognize these simple strongholds as the *Serious Symptoms* of a heart bondage. The brokenness that accompanies a heart bondage perpetuates the negative mind-sets which attract additional strongholds.

You might say that a heart bondage is the progenitor of simple strongholds. Most addictions, detrimental habits, dysfunctional lifestyles, and even infirmities are a result—or a Serious Symptom—of a heart bondage. When a person is enslaved to something, especially when that something is destructive, there is usually a heart bondage present. It remains a fact, however, that those without a heart bondage can also attain some detrimental habits, or simple strongholds. They are just not as apt to do so.

For the purposes of this discussion, I will clarify strongholds as falling into two categories: *simple strongholds* and *heart bondages*. If it's not a heart bondage, it's a simple stronghold. There are many varieties of simple strongholds, but there is only one kind of heart bondage.

One Size Fits All

All heart bondages are exactly the same. They may appear to differ, but indeed they do not. I picture them like a basic tool or device. If you have a toolbox full of standard combination locks which are all alike—same size, same brand—then you might consider them one-size-fits-all. Heart bondages are like that; they are one-size-fits-all. I do believe a heart bondage can get stronger through continued use and prolonged exposure to abuse—but not larger. They are not flexible, and they do not expand in any way.

The only thing that differentiates one heart bondage from another is the dictates, or instructions, imprinted on them. As we've seen, these go on at the time of abuse and reflect the nature of that activity. But the heart bondage on the one who suffered violence is *exactly the same* as the heart bondage on the one who suffered constant criticism. Only the instructions are different. The Serious Symptoms will vary, because of diverse personalities and variations in response to abuse, but the heart bondages are identical.

In one of my early Freedom Classes, a student shared with me her concerns. She said she was trying to figure out what kind of heart bondage she had. I explained that, although there are many different kinds of Serious Symptoms, there is only one type of heart bondage.

This is more good news! You don't have to configure any complicated formulas concerning your personal bondage issues. It should be a relief to know your heart bondage is the same as everyone else's—at least without considering the Serious Symptoms. Yours is not more elaborate than anyone else's, not more complex or difficult to resolve.

The knowledge we have about the heart bondage is simple and straightforward: *there's only one kind!* It is a wicked spiritual device with chains of shame and hopelessness, and its function is to rob a person of their true God-given identity. The Serious Symptoms do vary, but they are easily identifiable because you can see them.

> **The knowledge we have about the heart bondage is simple and straightforward: there's only one kind!**

There is nothing difficult about understanding a heart bondage, how it originates, or how it operates. We can recognize it as a tool of darkness, the source of much confusion and grief. And more importantly, we can gain insight on how to destroy it, because the Word of God tells us how to tear it down, step by step. I'm going to share that process with you, and I promise: *it's not complicated.*

One kind of heart bondage, one solution. *One answer.* The blood of Jesus Christ defeated death once and for all. And that includes the power of darkness over your mind.

Types of Strongholds

CHAPTER SIX WORKBOOK

TYPES OF STRONGHOLDS

1. What is a SIMPLE STRONGHOLD? Give three examples:

    1. _____
    2. _____
    3. _____

2. "All strongholds don't have to be from the devil." Why not?

3. Anyone can create a simple stronghold, even those who don't have a heart bondage. TRUE/FALSE

4. What are the three main distinctions between a HEART BONDAGE and a SIMPLE STRONGHOLD?

    1. _____
    2. _____
    3. _____

5. In the Workbook assignment for Chapter 5, Serious Symptoms, Question #3 (page 69), you made a list of Serious Symptoms you've experienced in your life. Now return to that list and note the age you were when you began exhibiting the behavior associated with each of those Symptoms.

6. A simple stronghold of gambling will result in a _____ habit.

7. As a student of freedom, you will recognize simple strongholds as the _____ _____ of a heart bondage.

8. A heart bondage is the progenitor of simple strongholds. TRUE/FALSE

9. "All heart bondages are exactly the same."

What is the only thing that differentiates one heart bondage from another?

10. Why does it APPEAR that there are many different kinds of heart bondages?

11. A heart bondage is a wicked spiritual device with chains of shame and hopelessness, and its function is to rob a person of their true God-given _____.

12. Understanding a heart bondage is:

    a. uncomplicated
    b. uncomplicated
    c. uncomplicated
    d. all of the above

BONUS QUESTION: Refer to your list of personal Serious Symptoms (See Question #5). Which of these tend to run in your family? Could these be a manifestation of a *generational curse*?

CHAPTER SEVEN

Scriptural Foundation

THE TERM *HEART BONDAGE* IS NOT USED BY THE WRITers of the scriptures. Rather, it is my own choice of terminology which accurately depicts a very real spiritual condition with very real consequences. While the term *heart bondage* is not in the Bible, the concept of the heart bondage most certainly is, and it's referred to as a "stronghold."

Sometimes scripture can sound a little formal, almost intimidating. A scriptural term (like "stronghold") is not particularly comfortable in everyday language. A more user-friendly term (like *heart bondage*) describes the condition perfectly. It is suitable for our conversation, like preferring jeans to a tuxedo. The term *heart bondage* is more relaxed, yet complies with the correct "stronghold" and is quite apt at getting to the heart of the matter.

This use of unstructured terminology is nothing new to the church. Other well-known religious terms are considered scripturally sound, yet are not the exact words used in the Bible. An excellent example of this is the word *rapture*, as referring to end-time prophecy. The Bible doesn't use the word "rapture." Yet the concept of the rapture is referred to in 1 Thessalonians 4:17, which uses the term "caught up." Christians the world over speak of this event as *the rapture*. They might say, "The rapture could happen any day." You don't usually hear, "The catching away could happen any day." The terminology believers are comfortable using—"the rapture"—is not explicitly scriptural. Still, the event described as *the rapture* is accurate. Believers are on point when they speak of the rapture.

Like that, the term *heart bondage* refers to an actual spiritual condition addressed in scripture. The Apostle Paul calls it "strongholds."

For the weapons of our warfare are not carnal but mighty in God for pulling down strongholds, casting down arguments and every high thing that exalts itself against the knowledge of God, bringing every thought into captivity to the obedience of Christ . . .
—**2 Corinthians 10:4–5 (NKJV)**

In this passage, the apostle raises the topic of "strongholds," then goes on to describe their location (in arguments, in the mind) and what they do (exalt themselves against the knowledge of God). In the original text, the word translated as "high thing" is *hupsoma*, which literally means *an elevated structure, a barrier, a rampart, a bulwark*. In another place in scripture, this same word is translated as *height*. These are self-elevated structures that come against the knowledge of God.

It interests me that these high things are self-elevated. ". . . *every high thing that exalts itself* . . ." They are not exalted by God or man, but only by the dark forces to which they belong. And there's a problem with that—a big problem, because they do not belong there. These high things are foreign. It is spiritually unlawful for anything from the darkness to take a prominent position in the mind of a believer.

The Apostle Paul leaves no doubt as to what we should do about these self-elevated structures. In short, they must be demolished. This "high thing" (strongholds) must be pulled down. The word translated in this verse as "pulling down" literally means *destruction* or *demolition*.

Pulling down depicts the activity of grabbing ahold and giving a firm tug. We must arrest these high things by removing them from the unlawful elevated position they have claimed, and putting them where they belong: under our feet (Romans 16:20). *Pull them down.*

There is something else quite interesting about this text. The term "strongholds" is plural (more than one), and "arguments" is plural (more than one). In the original text, the word used for "every" high thing is *pas*, which means "some of all types." In other words, there are different types of strongholds.

Of course, you already know this! You are well familiar with the many different kinds of strongholds. Alcoholism, drug addiction, uncontrolled anger, crippling depression, self-loathing, consuming jealousy, greed, verbal and emotional abuse, addiction to pornography, all detrimental habits—what we call *simple strongholds*—the list goes on and on. You can see it, and unbelievers can see it. If you still aren't sure, ask a psychologist, they'll tell you. They may not call it a "stronghold," they may call it something else. But we are all talking about the same thing: a firm grip on the mind by something unshakeable.

You don't have to be a biblical scholar to comprehend the concept of strongholds. Nor must you always have a scriptural foundation to identify conditions that exist in our world, here and now. Neither cancer, diabetes, nor heart disease is mentioned by name in the scriptures, yet we know they exist.

I believe it's safe to say the Bible is very general in identifying strongholds. When the Apostle Paul speaks on the subject, he doesn't mention the "stronghold of alcoholism" or the "stronghold of uncontrollable anger." He makes no distinction between types of strongholds.

However, we do make that distinction. As we observe and interact with others, we come to recognize those issues in people's lives. We call them *alcoholism, drug addiction, depression, eating disorders*, etc. The term *strongholds* is a generic term that can refer to any dysfunction fortified in the mind.

Yet there is a specific type of oppression that is in a class all its own. The Apostle Paul touches on it when he refers to the "arguments" and "every high thing" that exalts itself against the knowledge of God. This particular oppression originates in childhood because of abuse, neglect, or prolonged adverse conditions and is a progenitor of all other strongholds. Children who experience brokenness from these events will face an identity crisis that will eventually evolve into dysfunction on some level. Low self-worth, confusion, depression, and anxiety are always a companion to these grown-up kids.

This childhood-oriented "stronghold" is the kind we will target in this study. It's not a bondage to a substance or an addiction, nor is it a bondage to anything external. It's a bondage to the *thinking*, the "arguments" Paul mentions above. It's a bondage to the heart—thus the term *heart bondage*, which perfectly describes the inner work of this particular type of stronghold.

Spirit, Soul, Body

Believers suffer from emotional bondage just as nonbelievers do. This comes as a surprise to many Christians.

The word "freedom" is frequently used to describe the born-again status. Indeed, when one is born again, the new believer does attain immediate spiritual freedom. But *spiritual freedom* and *emotional freedom* are two different things. We should never assume that the born-again experience will result in automatic release from emotional bondage or that intense spiritual experiences will somehow banish all oppression.

You may be wondering how a believer could have a stronghold of any kind, heart bondage or otherwise. It may not make sense to think they could, especially if one has been saved for a while or served in a ministerial position. Yet many bound people are mature Christians who've had more than a few experiences with the Lord. They've sung songs about being free, talked about being free, and heard countless sermons about being free. If the truth sets us free, as Jesus said, and they've heard so much about it, then why are they still walking around with emotional chains? How could a heart bondage—or any kind of stronghold—stay attached through all that?

It does appear at first glance that all Christians should be free simply because they are what they are—*born-again believers*. However, we know this isn't the case. Not only is the raw reality of bondage evident

> **Believers suffer from emotional bondage just as nonbelievers do.**

in our congregations today, but we know the battle with strongholds was also a concern for believers in the early church. When the Apostle Paul wrote to the church in Corinth, he spoke of "our warfare" and "pulling down strongholds." (2 Corinthians 10:4) And these were New Testament Christians! Obviously, some of the believers at Corinth were struggling with bondage issues. We can conclude from Paul's letter that, if members of the early church could have strongholds in the first century, members of the church today can too.

Still, questions remain:

- Why do many believers suffer from emotional bondage when the Word promises freedom?

- Why doesn't the salvation experience eradicate a heart bondage?

- How does a heart bondage stay attached through salvation, water baptism, Holy Spirit baptism, and a myriad of other spiritual experiences?

The answer to these questions is quite simple, and it has a lot to do with how humans are designed.

Every person is composed of three parts: a spirit, a soul, and a body (1 Thessalonians 5:23). These three facets of mankind reflect the image of God, a divinity of three Persons: Father, Son, and Holy Spirit.

Let's take a closer look to see how each of these three parts of mankind relates to the heart bondage or strongholds of any type.

#1. The Human Spirit

The first part of man—the human spirit—is the innermost part. The spirit is eternal. It never dies. When you were born again, your spirit was instantly changed, transformed from the kingdom of darkness into the Kingdom of God.

> *He has delivered us from the domain of darkness and transferred us to the kingdom of his beloved Son, in whom we have redemption, the forgiveness of sins.*
> **—Colossians 1:13-14**

Your spirit is already "saved." There is no struggle in the spirit area, and you don't have to worry about making improvements on it. According to Ephesians 2:6, you are seated with Christ in the heavenly places. Your spirit has already made it to Heaven!

"God doesn't speak to your mind, He speaks to your spirit."
—Joel Osteen

#2. The Physical Body

The physical body is the outermost part, of course, and the easiest to locate. The body is not affected by the salvation experience at all. If a young man were tall and thin before he prayed the prayer of salvation, he'd be tall and thin afterward.

The physical body can reflect the spiritual condition, however. Through sickness and disease, violence, addictions, abuse, or neglect, the body can suffer from the effects of sin. It can also benefit from the impact of godliness through wholesome living, discipline, divine health, and divine healing.

> *Or do you not know that your body is a temple of the Holy Spirit within you, whom you have from God? . . .*
> **—1 Corinthians 6:19**

The physical body of the believer is the temple of the Holy Spirit. You should take care of your body and respect it as such. But no spiritual battles are fought in the natural arena. You don't fight spiritual battles with your physical body. The closest you'll come to fighting spiritual battles with your physical body is fasting.

#3. The Soul Region

Finally, there is the soul. Also known as the *heart*, this area is the battleground between good and evil. Comprised of the mind, the will, and the emotions, the heart is somewhat stuck in the middle. While the soul and the spirit are closely aligned, the soul is not altered by the salvation experience, as is the spirit. The heart is not automatically reborn, refashioned, or changed by a decision to follow Christ, or by any other spiritual event. Transformation is possible for the soul, however—but only through a renewal of the mind, which comes through time and intentional effort.

The soul, or the heart, is the location of all spiritual and emotional battles. That's why it's called the *battleground*. The struggle between light and darkness, good and evil, right and wrong, is waged in the soul region—in the mind, the will, and the emotions. The *flesh*, or the sin nature, resides in this area, giving rise to ungodly desires and temptations. Every dream is born and every decision is made in the mind.

> **The soul, or the heart, is the location of all spiritual and emotional battles. That's why it's called the battleground.**

Of the three parts of mankind, one is completely changed by salvation (the spirit); one is entirely untouched by it (the body); and one can go either way (the soul). The soul region is *neutral ground*.

There is one profound aspect of the soul region, or the heart: *The soul is where the heart bondage and all simple strongholds are attached.* This one simple fact is monumental in understanding the staying power of these tools of darkness.

A heart bondage will be unchanged by a decision to follow Christ or by most other spiritual experiences because it's in the wrong area for immediate transformation. Events that are spiritual in nature flow through the *spirit region, not the soul*, where the heart bondage resides.

Scriptural Foundation

The Three Parts of Mankind

SPIRIT: That part that is eternal.

- Transformed at salvation—a new creature in Christ!

- Needs no improvement

- The spirit does not struggle.

BODY: The easiest part to locate!

- Unchanged by the salvation experience.

- May reflect the effects of righteousness or sinful living through lifestyle.

- Does not fight spiritual battles.

SOUL: Also known as the *heart*. Comprised of the mind, the will, and the emotions.

- Is not transformed at salvation, but must be renewed.

- Where the flesh is located, the sin nature.

- This is the battleground!

That is why salvation does not immediately eradicate a heart bondage or other simple strongholds.

When a person receives salvation, any heart bondage or stronghold in residence will usually remain intact. The spirit has been changed, but not the soul—at least not yet. But there is hope! The area of the soul, or the heart, is still a candidate for transformation.

The heart can be trained in spiritual matters. It can be transformed to sustain a change in its nature, like remodeling the mind from unrighteousness to righteousness, from ungodliness to godliness, from foolishness to wisdom.

> **Do not be conformed to this world, but be transformed by the renewal of your mind, that by testing you may discern what is the will of God, what is good and acceptable and perfect.**
> **—Romans 12:2**

Getting saved is easy. But the real work begins after salvation! This is where you have to do your part. The Lord allows you—rather, He *requires* you—to be a participant in your own salvation by taking the initiative to transform your mind.

Although the soul is neutral ground, it is naturally carnal (unspiritual) by nature. You must train it to conform to the Word of God. Genuine heart change doesn't come easy, and you'll probably never get to the end of it because the flesh will always put up a fight. But still, it's your job to do. God won't do it for you. Your soul—your mind, your will, your emotions—*your heart*, is yours to manage.

Taking command of your mind is the opportunity of a lifetime. You have the chance (whether or not you want it) to take responsibility for your life, spiritually and otherwise. Your thoughts are yours, your habits are yours, your feelings are yours—and you have to deal with them. Most of your attitudes, opinions, and decisions are a response to the stress and pressures of life, and that is entirely a matter of the heart. Events that make one person strong and compassionate will make another cynical and bitter. You won't always be able to control your circumstances, but you can control how you respond to them. You can't blame anyone else for what goes on in your mind because no one else has command of it, only you.

Transforming the human heart into an instrument of righteousness is no small feat. It takes work, time, and perseverance. Renewing the mind is a lifelong process that involves changing mind-sets, adjusting attitudes, and keeping a check on desires. It's a matter of conforming the heart to the Word of God. In other words, we need to learn to *think like God thinks*.

But sometimes people don't know what to do because they aren't aware they lack wisdom. It's hard to seek answers when you don't even know the questions. A significant heart transformation will help us comprehend God's will and discern what is "good and acceptable and perfect." When we humble ourselves and pray for direction, the Holy Spirit will show us where we've been in error, lead us in the right direction, and help us change the way we think. He will fill in the gaps we didn't even know we had.

Getting "saved" doesn't solve all our immediate problems. It sets us in right standing with God and provides eternal security, yes—and thank God for that! But we need salvation in more than just one area. The spirit is transformed at salvation, but the soul must be transformed as well. If you allow your mind, will, and emotions to go unchecked and undisciplined, you will quickly find you're quite capable of carrying on just as you did before you were born again. Fleshly pursuits and bad habits will breed havoc and chaos in your life, no matter how long you've been a Christian.

One of the greatest mistakes believers can make is assuming the bulk of the spiritual work is behind them just because they've been born again. Eternal security is invaluable, but salvation is just the beginning. For those who call themselves the children of God, there is *so much more!*

CHAPTER SEVEN WORKBOOK

SCRIPTURAL FOUNDATION

1. Write out Colossians 1:13-14:

2. What does the Apostle Paul say we should do about strongholds?

3. Which of the following is a stronghold?

    a. alcoholism
    b. drug addiction
    c. low self-worth
    d. a heart bondage
    e. all of the above

4. What is the difference between a heart bondage and other strongholds?

5. "Spiritual freedom and emotional freedom are two different things." Why?

6. Every person is composed of three parts:

    1. _____
    2. _____
    3. _____

7. The soul, or the heart, is the location of all spiritual battles. That's why it's called the _____.

8. "The soul is where the heart bondage and all simple strongholds are attached."

    Why is this important?

9. Events which are spiritual in nature flow through the:

    a. spirit region
    b. body
    c. soul (the mind, will, and emotions)
    d. all of the above

10. Write out Romans 12:2:

11. The soul region (the mind, will, and emotions) is naturally carnal (unspiritual) by nature, but it can be trained in spiritual matters. TRUE/FALSE

12. "We need salvation in more than just one area. The spirit is transformed at salvation, but the soul must be transformed as well."

    What does it mean to TRANSFORM your mind? Why is it necessary?

BONUS QUESTION: We need to learn to think like _____ thinks.

CHAPTER EIGHT

The Truth Encounter

THERE ARE VARYING OPINIONS IN THE CHURCH COMmunity concerning how strongholds should be approached. One popular belief is that all bondage should be broken by prayer and the laying on of hands. Many hold the view that the *power* of God is all you need—and besides, it's so much faster than a process. *Why go to all this trouble to complete seven steps?*

Let me say that I absolutely believe in corporate prayer and the laying on of hands. The power of God is indeed strong enough to break any stronghold or bondage. I have seen it happen. This is known as a *power encounter*. However, I believe the power encounter is the exception, not the rule, for resolving most strongholds. Therefore we will not be using the power encounter to target the heart bondage.

In considering my reasons for this, let's review for a moment . . .

There are two basic kinds of strongholds: 1) heart bondages, and 2) simple strongholds. I believe *the vast majority of strongholds broken through a power encounter are simple strongholds*—not the heart bondage, which is our focus. But even when simple strongholds are removed by the sheer force of a power encounter, it is often a temporary solution. I witnessed an extraordinary example of this some years ago when a woman from my church went forward for prayer.

I knew Jane reasonably well, and I can say with confidence that she had a heart bondage. Jane had rock-bottom self-esteem and even less self-respect. She was grossly overweight, she stuttered severely, and she possessed not a thread of dignity. Jane once shared with me that her mother had tried to kill her when she was ten years old.

Despite all that, Jane was a faithful Christian. She loved the Lord and attended church regularly with her family. But Jane never seemed to expect a whole lot out of life. I'm sure she didn't expect the jaw-dropping miracle she received on the evening of her encounter.

There was a visiting minister in the house. Unusual events often happened in his services, and miracles were not uncommon. When the minister laid hands on Jane and prayed, she began to walk backward. Down the aisle, out through the foyer, and around the hallway that led back into the sanctuary, Jane made three large circles through the church. She laughed and walked backward the whole time. At the completion of the last round, Jane collapsed under the anointing of the Holy Spirit. When she got up, Jane no longer stuttered. I sat with Jane after service and talked with her about her experience as we shared a meal. She spoke as cohesively and as clearly as anyone.

What happened with Jane was an instant deliverance. She'd had a *power encounter*.

Was it a simple stronghold that was broken off of Jane that night, or was it the heart bondage? There's no way to know for sure, but I would guess it was a *simple stronghold*. The power of God broke the stronghold of fear that was on her mind and caused her to stutter. (Stuttering can be a Serious Symptom.) She was free, temporarily. But that's not the end of Jane's story.

Within a couple of weeks, Jane began to stutter again. It wasn't long before she was back in the same sad condition she was in before her deliverance.

Now, why did that happen? Why didn't Jane stay free?

First and foremost, Jane wasn't prepared for emotional freedom. You have to consider how she got to be bound in the first place. Strongholds and heart bondages are attached to people who are weak and vulnerable to attack by the enemy. Jane was, both before and after her miracle, emotionally weak and vulnerable. The power of God was enough, but she wasn't. Because of that, she could not prevent the enemy from a second attack. Jane was not strong enough to maintain her freedom.

> **The power of God is strong enough to break any stronghold, heal any disease, provide for any need, and make anyone whole.**

Sometime after Jane's event, I shared her story with one of my uncles, a minister of many years. Uncle Vernon listened intently, and then he had one question: *"Did she stay free?"* His question got my attention. He too had seen those who were instantly delivered revert back to their old ways in a matter of days.

The power of God is strong enough to break any stronghold, heal any disease, provide for any need, and make anyone whole. The problem is not with the power of God; *it is with us*.

In his magnificent book, *The Bondage Breaker,* Neil Anderson states, "Freedom from spiritual conflicts and bondage is not a power encounter; it's a truth encounter."[4]

A truth encounter.

There is tremendous power in truth. This liberating principle is overlooked by those who believe the power of God comes only through the electric experience of the instant manifestation.

It is tempting to look to the power encounter for answers. Those who have witnessed the awesome manifestation of God's power generally want more of it, and understandably so because it's something to desire. But some Christians come to believe this is where they'll get everything they need from God. They begin to lean into the power, often neglecting their emotional growth in the truth of God's Word. Unfortunately, this results in super-spiritual people who have holes in their character.

Too many power-packed believers walk out of the church doors, service after service, and head home to broken-down lives of failure and defeat—bad marriages, broken relationships, drama, overdrawn bank accounts, unbridled passions, weight problems, pornography addiction, low credit scores, questionable reputations, and the list goes on. Their

---

[4]. Neil T. Anderson. *The Bondage Breaker: Overcoming Negative Thoughts, Irrational Feelings, Habitual Since.* Harvest House. 2019.

lives are riddled with dysfunction and disorder, rendering them incapable of receiving the abundant life of which Jesus spoke. But because they have experienced the power of God, they think they're free. And on some level, they are. After all, there are various levels of freedom.

Do not make the mistake of believing a heart bondage (or any kind of stronghold) must fall in the wake of a strong manifestation of God's power. The flow of the anointing comes through the spirit region, not the soul, where the heart bondage and all simple strongholds are located. Even when the instant deliverance does happen—*and it does happen*—the bondage is almost certain to return if the person isn't emotionally and spiritually mature enough to maintain their newfound freedom.

All this is not to say that the body and the soul cannot experience and benefit from God's power; they can. Divine healing is an example of that. I personally have witnessed some miraculous healings. So allow me to stress again that the power encounter is a real thing. There's nothing more refreshing than a genuine move of the Holy Spirit. The power of God can touch and change any part of a person—spirit, soul, and body.

To be specific, the Apostle Paul did not say to remove strongholds by the laying on of hands. He said to *pull them down* and *cast them down* and *bring them into captivity* (2 Corinthians 10:4–5). The Word instructs believers to use the laying on of hands for certain purposes, but never specifically for deliverance. Nowhere in the Bible will you find that. Jesus dealt with demons by casting them out, but that is another matter. Demonic possession and heart bondages are two entirely different things. We are not dealing with demonic possession in this study.

Believers are to seek the truth in all things. It is the truth that will set you free.

. . . "If you abide in my word, you are truly my disciples, and you will know the truth, and the truth will set you free."
—John 8:31–32

So if you want power, you've got it. There is unparalleled power in the truth of God's Word. In this study, we will absolutely engage the power of God to attain emotional freedom, but it will come through *the power of the Truth*, and it will stick. When a truth encounter breaks that heart bondage, it will never come back, because *you will be changed.*

Remember what I said about the heart bondage being one-size-fits-all? And it is made of a type of material that looks like iron? A heart bondage is not flexible. It's static, and it doesn't expand, stretch, or grow with a person. But your soul can expand and grow. As you condition your mind to think like God thinks, and as you begin to walk in the fullness of the truth of God's Word, you'll grow and mature spiritually and emotionally, even in ways you haven't anticipated. You'll become a spiritual warrior, and soon that bondage won't be able to contain you. You'll outgrow that thing, and it will break. Those chains will absolutely fall off! When that happens, you won't have to worry about any old heart bondage ever coming back because it will no longer fit. You will have outgrown that wicked device, and you will be free for good!

There is a time for the power encounter. But no one has to pray for you, lay hands on you, or participate in any way for you to receive your emotional freedom. You don't have to wait for someone else to act, and you don't have to depend on someone else's faith. A truth encounter is between you and the Lord. There will never be a question as to who is responsible. It is God and God alone who will set you free.

Things a Heart Bondage Cannot Do

We've talked a lot about how a heart bondage attacks one's identity, initiates negative thought processes, and leads to detrimental lifestyle conditions. Now let's take a look at the things a heart bondage cannot do:

1) A heart bondage cannot change who you are.

The term "self-worth" refers to a sense of self, like a personal assessment. With your *self-worth*, you estimate your own value. Your actual worth, however, is not affected by your analysis or that of anyone else. Your real identity is who God says you are, and a heart bondage cannot change that.

No one can alter the original identity of any person because humans were created by God, the Creator. We were made in His image. We are all distinct individuals with a specific purpose on our life, endowed with gifts and talents that enable each of us to accomplish God's will and expand the Kingdom of God on the Earth. That's a done deal, and no one can do anything about it, not even you or me. God's plan is *the plan*.

The devil knows all this—probably better than we do. And he can't alter anyone's identity, either. Although he can't do anything about you or me and our awesome purpose, he can try to influence the way we see ourselves. He uses a heart bondage to help him do that. Satan hopes to distort our self-perception to derail us and get us off our designated course. This is the devil's game. The target is our thought processes.

> *Your real identity is who God says you are. That's a done deal, and no one can do anything about it, not even you or me.*

It's all a big smokescreen. Remember that a heart bondage consists of lies; there's no truth in any of it. The enemy cannot alter your real identity, nor can anyone else.

2) A heart bondage cannot affect your salvation.

The presence of a heart bondage does not in any way affect your standing with Heaven. Many sincere Christians have served God faithfully with a heart bondage intact. Teachers, deacons, praise leaders, Spirit-filled believers, Sunday school teachers, even pastors—people in every area of the church community—can and do have heart bondages. It doesn't mean they are not as committed as other Christians, love God any less, or have questionable character. It certainly doesn't mean they are lacking in faith.

Now that you are aware of the heart bondage, you can go about the business of getting free. Whatever you do, you must not allow the enemy to pressure you into doubting your salvation. In no way does a heart bondage threaten your security in Christ.

3) A heart bondage cannot deprive you of God-given gifts and talents.

The presence of a heart bondage does not affect gifts and talents. Your gifts are a portion of your personal truth, a part of your authentic identity. Again, a heart bondage attempts to lie to you about who you are, but it cannot change who you are. Gifts and talents are part of the real you, and they are unaffected.

4) A heart bondage cannot affect your anointing.

Every Christian should have a ministry of some kind. With that ministry comes an *anointing*. The word *anointing* means one is *chosen and empowered by God* to do a specific thing.

The anointing is closely associated with gifts. If gifted in an area, you will receive an anointing that empowers you to accomplish more with that gift through the grace of God. If you are gifted, you will be anointed; if you are anointed, you will be gifted. People tend to associate the anointing with ministry gifts, but the anointing isn't just for the pulpit. You can be anointed in cooking, caring for children, business, or for the medical field. It's what you do well—*your gift*. You can be gifted and anointed in more than one area.

When one allows the Lord to use their gifts and anointing for His glory, they have a *ministry*. The distinctive characteristic of a ministry is the anointing; that's what makes it different from other similar activities. When the anointing of the Holy Spirit is on it, the power of God will be in it. Lives are changed through the most humble acts when the power of God is present.

It is both a privilege and an obligation for believers to embrace their anointing and serve accordingly. When they do, they are in essence serving both God and others. In this way, the church greatly impacts the world as the hands and feet of Jesus Christ on the Earth today—loving, serving, engaging, giving.

If there is one group of Christians who has trouble admitting they have a heart bondage, it's the super-spiritual ones. Often leaders in the church community, those of strong faith sometimes have a difficult time grasping the possibility that they could have a stronghold of any kind

> **It is both a privilege and an obligation for believers to embrace their anointing and serve accordingly.**

because of the anointing that's on their lives. Those who serve in ministry are particularly apt to question their vulnerability to emotional injury. This is typical, even if they struggle with damaged self-worth and display various other Serious Symptoms.

A heart bondage cannot in any way hinder the anointing or a flow of the Spirit of God. Like simple strongholds, a heart bondage is located in the soul region, while the anointing and spiritual experiences flow through the spirit region. Your anointing is God's gift to you. It is the power of God on your life and is untouched by a heart bondage.

5) A heart bondage does not diminish your potential for success and achievement.

The presence of a heart bondage always makes life more difficult. However, emotional brokenness does not prevent life from happening, and those with a heart bondage can be high achievers. Though a heart bondage causes overall identity confusion and can affect one's entire life because of damaged self-worth, it will usually manifest itself predominantly *in one particular area* of a person's life. (This is where the Serious Symptoms show up.) But that doesn't mean a broken person cannot be successful—even at times in the area in which they experience some dysfunction.

For example, a man may have a lucrative business but be verbally abusive to his wife and children. Another person may have excellent personal relationships but remain under the poverty level because they believe they aren't smart enough to hold a good job. A woman may be quite intellectual, yet unable to manage areas of her personal life because of sexual dysfunction.

The ever-present challenge to one's self-worth will often affect every area of life to some degree. But people can overcome great difficulty when using their gifts and talents in doing what they do best. The power of the anointing cannot be overrated, as it enables people to accomplish extraordinary things they could never manage in their own strength.

Some of the world's most prominent and influential figures have been exceptional people with a heart bondage. If I were to attach a list of well-known personalities I suspect had a heart bondage, you'd be shocked. The world has been shaped by those who suffered from childhood trauma. Most certainly, Winston Churchill was one. His biography tells of a little boy who begged his parents to visit him at school, but they never had time for their son. Winston grew up lonely. He saved the world from tyranny, yet remarkably, he suffered from depression all his life.

Some might assume that heart bondages are more predominant among the poor and uneducated. That is not exactly true. The influence of dysfunction stemming from generational curses can have a negative effect on the economic and educational achievement in families. However, the power of money and prestige is not a comprehensive solution to brokenness. Prosperity may provide a more affluent lifestyle and hide a lot of deficiencies, but it cannot heal a heart broken in childhood. The tool of the kingdom of darkness that we call a *heart bondage* is nondiscriminatory; it makes no distinction between people. That includes all the children of God: both men and women, rich and poor, all races, and all communities.

Finding a Solution

The end of this chapter concludes our close examination of the heart bondage. I trust that you now have some comprehension of the vicious cycle a heart bondage presents. I hope you know what our enemy is about, the immeasurable cruelty in which he thrives, and what he has planned for mankind. *What he has planned for your life.*

It is important to apprehend the nature of our opponent and to be aware of his tactics. In the last few chapters, we have scrutinized a lot of dark things by carefully observing the heart bondage and investigating the enemy's strategies. We must embrace our newfound insight because *remaining in a bound condition is not a viable option.* Understanding the mechanics of a heart bondage will help us to win in the end.

Tony Robbins said, "Identify your problems, but give your power and energy to solutions." Now we will do exactly that. We will direct our power and energy to find answers. It is time to shift our focus: *from the problem to the solution.* What do we do about a heart bondage? How is a heart bondage removed? Can a bound person ever be totally free?

Yes! There is a way out, and I'm excited to share it with you. Let's continue to Part 2, where we discuss the answers to these questions and more.

CHAPTER EIGHT WORKBOOK

THE TRUTH ENCOUNTER

1. What is a POWER ENCOUNTER?

2. What is a TRUTH ENCOUNTER?

3. The flow of the anointing comes through the spirit region, not the soul, where the heart bondage and all simple strongholds are located. TRUE/FALSE

4. Write out John 8:31-32:

5. There is unparalleled power in the truth of God's _____.

6. How does one outgrow a heart bondage?

7. A heart bondage cannot affect or change:

    a. your true identity
    b. your salvation
    c. your God-given gifts and talents
    d. your anointing
    e. your potential for success and achievement
    f. all of the above

8. Why does the devil try to alter a person's PERCEPTION of their own identity?

9. "Many sincere Christians have served God faithfully with a heart bondage intact. Teachers, deacons, praise leaders, Spirit-filled believers, Sunday school teachers, even pastors—people in every area of the church community—can and do have heart bondages."

    How is this possible?

10. Do you believe there is an anointing on your life? Explain.

11. A heart bondage is nondiscriminatory, and it makes no distinction between people. That includes both men and women, rich and poor, all races, and all communities. TRUE/FALSE

12. Why is it important that we understand the devil's tactics?

🔥 🔥 🔥

BONUS QUESTION: "Remaining in a bound condition is not a viable option."

Explain why this is true, and what it means to you.

PART 2

The Journey

CHAPTER NINE

The Power of a Testimony

THE WORD *TESTIMONY* IS DEFINED AS AN AFFIDAVIT OR an affirmation. It is a witness or a declaration, a statement of evidence. My own testimony is an account of how God set me free from the bonds of shame and hopelessness. I use my story as a prototype for the freedom process. It's an example, a model to follow—a *prototype*.

Broken people often feel isolated and alone. They believe they cannot share how they feel, that no one would understand. An overwhelming sense of detachment prevails with the conviction that they're the only one who suffers from such confusion.

Hearing my story helps people to relate. It breaks down barriers and brings hope, enabling people to see they are not alone in their affliction. *If God can do that for her, then maybe He can do that for me.*

> *And they overcame him by the blood of the Lamb, and by the word of their testimony; and they loved not their lives unto the death.*
> —Revelation 12:11 (KJV)

Here is a promise that believers can and will overcome the enemy. The blood of Jesus is central to our story, as it was the blood that purchased our salvation and provided for our healing and deliverance. Everything we need for corporate and personal victory is provided by the blood of Jesus Christ.

According to this scripture passage, however, there is a second element that is a factor in overcoming: *the word of their testimony*.

It would appear from this passage that a testimony is a powerful tool, a means to overcome the enemy. Now that's saying something! And all along, you thought your story wasn't worth telling . . .

Everyone has a testimony; you have one. Your testimony is your story, the statement of your life, where you've been and where you are now, and what God has done for you. It's not meant to be held a secret but shared. Although your testimony is never a finished work until your days on Earth are done, it's a valuable commodity at any given point in time. Your story can be used to bless and encourage others even when you know God isn't finished with you yet. You don't have to have your act perfectly together to have a testimony of value.

When we have a need, quite often God will give the answer to someone else. The thing we're searching for—*our solution*—is given to another so they can pass it on. When we receive our answer from that other person, we're really receiving it from God, as He is the ultimate Giver, but we get it from the person who happens to be holding what we need.

Why would God choose to provide this way? Why doesn't He just deal with us all individually?

Because *God is a God of relationship*. He's a God of *community*.

> **Your story can be used to bless and encourage others even when you know God isn't finished with you yet.**

Community is a much needed element in the church today, one that has been neglected somewhat in recent years. Community requires a group, and it involves sharing. It speaks of coming together and personally experiencing the dynamic that is characteristic of camaraderie, of being a part of something bigger than oneself. People in a vibrant community react with one another and care for one another. They encourage each other. This is absolutely the perfect will of God regarding His people.

> **And let us consider how to stir up one another to love and good works, not neglecting to meet together, as is the habit of some, but encouraging one another, and all the more as you see the Day drawing near.**
> **—Hebrews 10:24–25**

God wants you in relationship with Him, and He wants you in relationship with others. But what does this have to do with your testimony, exactly?

Notice in the above scripture the phrases, "stir up one another" and "encouraging one another." What better way to speak encouragement to another than by sharing your own story of struggle and perseverance? If you have been in a battle and lived to tell it—even if you are still in the middle of it—you have something to say.

Yes, I know you probably have your objections. For starters, let's look at what you may already be thinking:

- I'm still struggling, and I'm not sure how my own story is going to turn out.
- I'm not an expert in anything.
- I don't consider myself an overcomer just yet. I'm not that spiritual.
- Who is going to listen to me anyway?
- My story is not dramatic enough.

Your story doesn't have to be perfect, and you don't have to be perfect, to share your testimony with others as a means of encouragement. Nor does your experience have to be overly dramatic. My own story is a good example of that. I've been privileged to hear the testimonies of many of my students, some of whom depict horrific childhood experiences that were foreign to me. My own story is not nearly as dramatic, but it is still relatable. Never judge the impact of your witness by comparing it with the experience of someone else.

The biggest hurdle for most is that their story is still a work in progress. The argument that the struggling person doesn't have the right to claim a testimony is just another of the enemy's tactics to keep believers silent. When you think about it, the blessed fact that some people are still here is a witness to God's goodness. Just because your story isn't finished is no reason to be quiet about what God has done for you so far. Your story will continue to unfold as long as your feet walk this Earth. If you have to wait until your testimony is complete, you'll have to wait until you're dead. So at what point do you think you'll feel confident to start sharing?

God created you to be a part of a community. You need other people, and people need you. That is God's way of doing things. None of us are entirely self-sufficient. How can we in good conscience each go our own way with our Bible tucked neatly under our arm, blissfully ignoring the cries of those around us, when we suspect that we do, perhaps, have solutions?

If the Lord gave us our answers individually, we would each have our needs met, but we might not reach out to other people. We would have a relationship with our Heavenly Father, but we might not need anyone else. People needing people is the essence of community and family. Can you imagine how you would feel if you were a parent and your children didn't interact? If they never had anything to say to each other, except perhaps an occasional text?

> **God created you to be a part of a community.
> You need other people, and people need you.
> That is God's way of doing things.**

Community is all about relationship, people loving people. What better way to reach out than with your own story of struggle and triumph, joy and sadness, hope and endurance—*your experience?*

"I've been where you are," says a lot to a hurting soul. "God got me out, and He will do the same for you" offers hope like nothing else.

The Prototype

My testimony is a witness to God's grace. It's a demonstration that can be used as a pattern to receive your own freedom. Once you've heard about my experience, you have the opportunity to do what I did. You can follow my testimony and take the path I took that leads to lasting emotional freedom. What God did once (for me), He will do again (for you.)

During the course of my life, I was unaware that I needed anything like a deliverance. I knew the Bible makes mention of strongholds, but I certainly didn't think I had one. I thought I was too religious for that. (Yes, I'd had a vision of chains on my heart during my college freshman year, but I didn't make the connection.) Heart bondages operate in secret, so like others bound by shame, I was clueless. I lived the days of my life dragging the weight of damaged self-worth and a dreadful sense of hopelessness, even as I struggled to make sense of things that made no sense.

I was what some would call a *fighter*. The truth is, I was a *survivor*. I did my best to figure life out. I was somewhat educated, tried to live right, and experienced some success simply because I worked so hard. I loved serving God and my family. But matters became critical just when I should have been reaping the harvest of my life's efforts, and all I could see was failure.

Then one day, during a Fourth of July weekend, something happened that caused me to stop in my tracks and make a decision for change. Faced with defeat, I had to concede that things weren't going to work out the way I had hoped. I could no longer continue the way I was going. I didn't know exactly what I was going to do, but I did know that change had to happen, and it had to start with me—not my address, not my kids, not my bank account, not even my marriage—but *with me*. That is the day I began the journey that would change my life.

I began that journey with some decisions. These decisions were *heart changes* that had nothing to do with my unsettling circumstances, the external conditions of my life, or with anyone else—but *they had everything to do with me.* I didn't have control over most of my circumstances, but I did have control over what went on between my ears. I met head-on those challenges I had evaded for decades, matters which required straightforward adjustments in my attitudes and perceptions. That included the way I thought about things—life, circumstances, people. The way I viewed myself. As I made these adjustments, I determined not to waiver from my newfound perspectives but to allow my new thought patterns to take hold.

This is where God showed up. Never before had I been capable of generating inner change. I knew this all too well, as I had just spent several decades struggling with a heaviness I could only describe as a "ball and chain." Yet suddenly—and unexpectedly—inner change did begin to occur, all as a result of some very simple decisions.

That which I had never been able to do through my own strength, I was suddenly able to do through the power of God in me. This paradigm shift occurred when I humbled myself, got my heart right, and became obedient to the Lord. It happened when I gave up on doing things my way and started doing things God's way. Learning to think as God thinks was the simple measure that opened my heart and allowed divine intervention to correct my thought processes. If I may emphasize the point, *it was my manner of thinking that was my problem all along*—nothing more, nothing less.

Acquiring new mental habits was a fluid process, never static, and it affected me in ways I could not have imagined. As I allowed the Lord to correct my damaged thought processes, I kept changing, evolving, and growing. Those new thought patterns, once established, presented an opportunity for even more change, inviting new challenges, involving more decisions.

The challenges came, one after the other, as I followed the Lord's lead. I met every challenge with dauntless faith, the kind of courage one can possess when they have nothing left to lose. I knew how the Lord wanted me to respond to each challenge and, although afraid at times, I complied with explicit obedience. As I allowed the internal changes to transform my thoughts and, even more importantly, my thought patterns, the Lord led me from one challenge to the next. Each challenge, each decision, was higher than the one before, a step up. It was a *process*, and the result was dynamic emotional growth.

The heart decisions I made in response to each challenge were not always easy, nor were they incredibly difficult. They were all made in obedience to divine guidance and resulted in an inner transformation, which changed *me*. I felt I was growing and becoming stronger, aware of a continual sense of peace. The confusion that had been a constant companion began to dissipate. Soon I was presented with a very unexpected development: the way I viewed myself had changed! I no longer considered myself a nothing and a nobody, and I was beginning to believe that perhaps I did indeed matter.

Then one morning, the chains fell off. In an instant, Jesus Christ set me free from the bondage of shame and hopelessness. To say that this event came as a complete surprise is an understatement of epic proportions.

I'd had no idea! I hadn't realized that I was headed toward a deliverance, because I didn't know I was bound. At one point, I did sense that something extraordinary was happening, that the Lord was taking me somewhere; I just didn't know where. The challenges and decisions I'd met were, unbeknownst to me, milestones of courage with significant consequence. And although I was not fully aware of the growth I was making in the emotional arena, I reveled in my new experiences with the Lord. For the first time ever, this believer truly gave her life fully to Jesus Christ.

When the chains finally did break off, I instantly knew what had happened. I recognized the chains as those which had bound me as an eight-year-old girl. For one who was oblivious to God's methods and intentions, I think that is a miracle in itself.

We do indeed serve a God of surprises!

I consider it a great privilege to share with you the process which set me free. You have the exciting opportunity to seek emotional freedom deliberately and with your eyes wide open, as you follow my testimony. I believe what God did for me, He will do for you.

It is with great pleasure that I introduce you to The Freedom Class.

Introducing: The Freedom Class

Translating my experience into a curriculum others can follow gave birth to The Freedom Class. The process of change and emotional growth is termed *the journey*. Each challenge, or decision, is a *step*, with seven sequential steps to the journey. I have carefully replicated my experience so others can walk through the journey in confidence that what God did for me, He will do for them. In The Freedom Class, I will teach you to walk through the steps exactly as I did.

Immediately upon receiving my freedom, I felt impressed to write my experiences of the past few months. I heard the Lord say, "Look back." I responded immediately, journaling my recent history beginning on the day in my laundry room. I recorded the challenges I had encountered, the decisions I'd made, and the events which followed.

Writing what would eventually become my testimony, a sequence of actions seemed to lift off the page. It was clear the Lord had led me through a *walking out* process—walking out of the bondage. I could see where I had started making changes, and why it was so important when I made the hard decisions. I saw the moves I had made—a turn here, a step there—during those months of intense fellowship with Him. I began to comprehend how He had taken me by the hand and, even in my blind and broken condition, walked me through the process that leads to emotional freedom.

I am sharing this part of my story because I want you to understand that I didn't do any of this myself. I was totally helpless and completely clueless. I didn't know enough about my broken condition even to pray the prayer of faith to be set free. *It was all God*. I can't take credit for any of it. I can claim that I was obedient, but even that was by divine grace.

When it's all God, you've got something. God's plans don't fail. His methods are sure. If it were Debbie's plan, then I wouldn't be quite so certain. But I can assure you in confidence that the process in The Freedom Class works because it's God's way all the way, and it's incredibly simple.

In The Freedom Class, I will take you by the hand and walk you through the process that leads to lasting emotional freedom. That's precisely what God did for me, and now I am going to do it for you. I have been there, so I can take you there. I have walked a particular path, so I

> **With your willing participation, by the power of the Holy Spirit, He can and will accomplish His purposes in you through the truth of His Word.**

can show you how to walk that path. God's Word works for everybody. *Just as it worked for me, it will work for you.*

Follow my testimony. I will use it consistently as we walk through each step, unfolding my story in more detail as we go along. Allow me to share with you the incredible power of truth that will amaze you in its simplicity and effectiveness.

During the process, I will never tell you to do anything that is not soundly scriptural. Every step is based on the Word of God. Much of it you may have heard before, but it is imperative that you do not tweak the process to suit preexisting beliefs or assumptions. Just do it as I did it.

I want to make it clear from the outset that I cannot set you free. I can lead you to freedom, but only God can deliver you from the bondage of shame and hopelessness. With your willing participation, by the power of the Holy Spirit, He can and will accomplish His purposes in you through the truth of His Word.

I have had the joyous opportunity of leading others to freedom and seeing their testimonies become a living witness to my own story. The process works because it's God's way of setting people free. I believe the time is right for the church to get in shape to influence the world, and the first order of business is freedom from the past.

Later on, I'll tell you more about The Freedom Class and how to get started. But first, I'd like to share with you some fundamental principles we use in this study as we endeavor to comprehend the concepts of emotional bondage and deliverance. These truths of God's Word lay a foundation of wisdom and understanding that will help us better to embrace change and anticipate the accompanying struggle—and teach us how to employ God's power in our lives as we reach for the abundant life, ultimately defeating the bondage of shame and hopelessness, the heart bondage.

CHAPTER NINE WORKBOOK

THE POWER OF A TESTIMONY

1. What is a TESTIMONY?

2. Write out Revelation 12:11:

3. According to the above scripture (Question #2), there are TWO ELEMENTS involved in overcoming. They are:

   1. _____
   2. _____

4. Your story can bless and encourage others even when you know God isn't finished with you yet. TRUE/FALSE

5. God wants us to need and interact with other people because He is a God of _____ and _____.

6. Write out Hebrews 10:24–25:

7. To share your story effectively, you should wait until:

   a. you get baptized
   b. you are perfect
   c. you get your act together
   d. you are dead
   e. none of the above

8. Whose testimony have you read/heard that has encouraged and touched you significantly? (Someone you actually know, or someone you've met. Not a celebrity.) Why?

9. God can use your testimony, even when:

a. you're still struggling and don't know how things are going to turn out
   b. you're not an expert
   c. you're not a spiritual leader
   d. you think your story is boring or not very dramatic
   e. all of the above

10. What objections come to mind when you think about using your story to encourage others?

    How can you overcome these objections?

11. If you were to share your story with others, what do you think would happen?

12. "The process in The Freedom Class works because it's God's way all the way."

    Why is it important that we seek emotional freedom GOD'S WAY?

🔥 🔥 🔥

BONUS QUESTION: Copy this sentence:

I can use Debbie's story as an example to receive my own freedom. What God did for her, He will do for me.

CHAPTER TEN

The Full Armor of God

WE WILL BE USING A WIDE RANGE OF BIBLICAL TEXTS during this study. But one we will return to again and again is a passage in Ephesians 6 about *putting on the Full Armor of God*.

> *[10] Finally, be strong in the Lord and in the strength of his might. [11] Put on the whole armor of God, that you may be able to stand against the schemes of the devil. [12] For we do not wrestle against flesh and blood, but against the rulers, against the authorities, against the cosmic powers over this present darkness, against the spiritual forces of evil in the heavenly places. [13] Therefore take up the whole armor of God, that you may be able to withstand in the evil day, and having done all, to stand firm. [14] Stand therefore, having fastened on the belt of truth, and having put on the breastplate of righteousness, [15] and, as shoes for your feet, having put on the readiness given by the gospel of peace. [16] In all circumstances take up the shield of faith, with which you can extinguish all the flaming darts of the evil one; [17] and take the helmet of salvation, and the sword of the Spirit, which is the word of God, [18] praying at all times in the Spirit, with all prayer and supplication . . .*
> —Ephesians 6:10–18

We will approach this passage in small segments, like point destinations on a map. If we do indeed have a map for our journey, this passage is it. Ephesians 6 is the key—and the guide—to our destination.

The warrior in this passage represents *the believer*. Like the warrior, we can be "strong in the Lord and in the strength of His might" by clothing ourselves in the Full Armor of God. The Armor is detailed for us as seven separate pieces.

1. The Belt of Truth
2. The Breastplate of Righteousness
3. The First Shoe
4. The Second Shoe
5. The Shield of Faith
6. The Helmet of Salvation
7. The Sword of the Spirit

The Full Armor serves the purpose of protecting, maturing, and strengthening the believer. Verse 11 tells us to put on the Full Armor of God so we may be able to "stand against the schemes of the devil." The word "schemes" in the original Greek text is *methodeias*, which means *methods*. According to my Dake Bible, *methodeias* refers to the "different means, plans, and schemes used to deceive, entrap, enslave, and ruin the souls of men."[5]

Well, I don't think it could get any plainer than that. But there is more!

According to Verse 12, the perpetrators of these methods and schemes are not mortal beings of flesh and blood, but they are *rulers* and *authorities* of an unseen world. They are "cosmic powers over this present darkness" and "spiritual forces of evil" whose methods are invisible to the natural eye, so most people are unaware they even exist—although they will undoubtedly feel the effects of them at times. But you must know that these dark methods and schemes are not natural weapons.

A heart bondage is definitely a *methodeias*. It's a fortress of shame built in the mind of a child at an early age, with the evil intent to gain

---

5. Finis Jennings Dake. *Dake's Annotated Reference Bible*, Copyright © 1963, 1991, 212.

control of their thought processes. When the enemy manages to manipulate one's thoughts, he can gain some control over their behavior, inflicting hopelessness and seeking destruction through the bound person's own participation. You'll possibly recognize this pattern in some people when you observe the lives of those around you. We don't always have to know a person well to recognize the presence of a heart bondage.

Perhaps the enemy has other tools at his discretion, but the heart bondage must be one of his favorites. That's obvious by merely observing the vast number of people that have them.

The enemy's campaign against humanity is *strategic*. When you carefully study the Ephesians passage on the Full Armor of God, that fact becomes apparent. Satan's attacks are not haphazard, not the product of a carelessly planned, half-baked effort—but they are "flaming darts" aimed with precision. If you've ever thought the devil strikes randomly, just hoping to throw a punch on occasion, you must reconsider. Satan has been a student of human psychology for a long time, and he is very good at what he does.

I am not of the mind to glorify the enemy—he is, after all, a *defeated foe*. However, I encourage you to take him seriously because of his incredible stealth and ability to persuade and deceive. This enemy of yours once tried to overthrow God's throne, started a war in Heaven, and when he got kicked out, took a third of the angels with him. Given half an opportunity, he is quite capable. The Apostle Peter described the devil as "a roaring lion, seeking someone to devour." (1 Peter 5:8).

The question arises: *How do we put on the Full Armor of God?* We are talking about spiritual weapons that are symbolic, yet represent actual concepts that have very real implications in our daily lives. Ephesians 6, depicting the Roman warrior, is a beautiful passage that has contributed to many texts and sermons rich in lofty ideals. But without a working knowledge of the application of those ideals, you get *religion*, which can inspire but never liberate, educate but never empower. We must embrace the content of this passage in such a way that it will confront the brokenness in our lives and bring real change.

Putting on the Full Armor of God means to be *fully armed with the Word*. Some might assume that means knowing a lot of scripture. But we must concede that knowledge alone cannot be the definition of spiritual maturity. The practice of confessing and claiming scripture is employed by multitudes of Christians, a great many who have virtually no power and display all the evidence of a heart bondage. Possessing a broad knowledge of scripture is a good thing. Still, familiarity with scripture is not enough to win the victory over the enemy's tactics. This is evidenced by the multitudes of believers who are versed in the Word, yet live broken lives.

The term "put on" speaks of *application*. We must utilize the Word of God in both practical and spiritual means in order to incorporate real change. It's easy to get it between your ears—but you must get it in your heart. And that's the challenge with the truth: how to get it from your head down into your heart. It's the truth you *apply to your life* that will set you free.

Ephesians 6 gives us an illustration of *dressing ourselves in spiritual garments*. It's a picture of application. Notice that the scripture commands us to dress ourselves; God won't do it for us. But what might appear to be difficult (getting the Word from our head to our heart) becomes easy when we do it God's way.

Getting dressed is a process. We don't jump into all our clothes at once. In that same way, applying the Word to our life is a process as well, one which happens in layers. Putting on the Full Armor of God is a matter of growth. The Apostle Paul calls it a *transformation*. Each piece of the Full Armor unfolds a new revelation of who we are in Christ and opens doors for more levels of intimacy with God. This is the growth—and the process—that leads to emotional freedom.

> **We must utilize the Word of God in both practical and spiritual means in order to incorporate real change. It's the truth you apply to your life that will set you free.**

The Full Armor of God must be put on *in the order directed*. Ephesians 6 gives us that order, starting with the Belt of Truth. There is a reason for this precision: It's God's way of doing things. And we will not attempt

[13] Therefore take up the whole armor of God, that you may be able to withstand in the evil day, and having done all, to stand firm.

[14] Stand therefore, having fastened on the belt of truth, and having put on the breastplate of righteousness,

[15] and, as shoes for your feet, having put on the readiness given by the gospel of peace.

[16] In all circumstances take up the shield of faith, with which you can extinguish all the flaming darts of the evil one;

[17] and take the helmet of salvation, and the sword of the Spirit, which is the word of God,

[18] praying at all times in the Spirit, with all prayer and supplication . . .

EPHESIANS 6:13-18

to do it any other way because, quite frankly, we would be foolish to try. If the Lord says to put on the Full Armor a certain way, that's how we need to put it on. We do, after all, want to get the maximum benefit from our efforts. I cannot express enough the importance of proceeding according to God's order. We can never outdo, hurry up, or improve God's methods by instituting our own plans and preferences.

Notice that in the Ephesians 6 passage, the warrior is *standing*. He isn't hitting, jabbing, jumping, running, or even fighting; he is standing. The word "stand" or "withstand" is mentioned four times in this passage. It appears the warrior (the believer) is maintaining his position simply by standing on the Word of God. To those who have no faith left in themselves, this is a great comfort. So many people have tried to overcome the darkness on their own and failed. Discouraged and disheartened, even to the point of giving up all hope, they may feel they don't have any fight left. But when you've lost confidence in yourself, you can renew your faith in God. It's His strength, His might, and His truth that destroy the chains of bondage and set the captives free. As you stand on the Word of God, the Lord will go to battle on your behalf.

Emotional And Spiritual Growth

The Freedom Class details putting on the Full Armor of God to attain lasting emotional freedom through *spiritual and emotional growth*. The process will strengthen and mature you as a believer, enabling you to fight the good fight of faith with confidence. It's about your identity, plain and simple, and transforming the broken thought processes which bring confusion in that area. When you outgrow the identity crisis, you will outgrow the heart bondage. There's nothing more to it than that.

The seven steps of The Freedom Class are aligned precisely with the seven pieces of the Full Armor of God, and there are detailed instructions for the application of each. As you complete the first step, you will put on the first piece of armor, the Belt of Truth. As you take the second step, you will put on the second piece of armor, the Breastplate of Righteousness, and so on. In this way, you'll engage in dynamic spiritual warfare that results in spiritual and emotional maturity.

Interestingly, the Full Armor of God is not the only spiritual clothing mentioned in scripture. It does, however, have its own distinction. Some other garments in the Bible are the robe of righteousness, the clothing of salvation, and the garment of praise. These are available to all believers, regardless of their level of spiritual maturity. Not so for the Full Armor. One cannot put on the Full Armor of God and remain a baby Christian.

As weapons go, some are offensive, and some are defensive. The first six pieces in the Full Armor of God are for *defensive purposes*. They are for *protection*, although they may have some limited offensive properties. When you put on these first six pieces of armor, you will be going about the business of getting your heart right, seeking God's face, and discovering the mysteries of the Kingdom of God. These prepare you for the seventh and final step: taking up the Sword of the Spirit, which is where the power is. The Sword is the only offensive weapon of the warrior.

We can never utilize the Sword until we are prepared to handle it. Wielding the power of the Sword requires maturity, so we have to grow some, and we have to learn some things. That's why babies and children aren't allowed to play with knives. The Sword is mentioned last because it's at the highest level of maturity. Swords are for warriors.

Spiritual and emotional growth, like natural growth, take time. You must give yourself the time you need to embrace the process. The seven steps of The Freedom Class are very simple and straightforward. Simple doesn't always mean easy however, and there will be times when you'll have to stretch yourself a bit to reach the next level. There will be some hard decisions to make. But there's nothing complicated about the Word of God. If it's complicated, it's probably not God.

Spiritual and emotional maturity is the solution to resolving a complex identity crisis. Putting on the Full Armor of God is the essence of transformational change. Maybe you've heard sermons and lectures on the Full Armor of God, and you're wondering what I've got to say that's

> **Putting on the Full Armor of God is the essence of transformational change.**

different. I can promise, you have never heard it quite the way I teach it. I'll make it easy. You just need to know exactly how it's done!

When we think *armor*, we tend to think *kingdom*. That's logical, as one who wears a suit of armor usually identifies as a warrior associated with an army. If we are to then put on the Full Armor of God and dress like warriors, we must belong to a Kingdom. As it turns out, we do! As a child of God and disciple of Jesus Christ, you already know the King. But how much do you know about the Kingdom to which you belong? Well, let's investigate. You'll love everything about it because it's *the greatest Kingdom ever!*

CHAPTER TEN WORKBOOK

THE FULL ARMOR OF GOD

1. See Ephesians 6:10–18. List the seven pieces of the Full Armor of God below:

    1. _____
    2. _____
    3. _____
    4. _____
    5. _____
    6. _____
    7. _____

2. In Ephesians 6, the warrior represents the _____.

3. The Full Armor of God serves the purpose of:

    a. protecting the believer
    b. maturing the believer
    c. strengthening the believer
    d. all of the above

4. The methods and schemes of the devil are unseen to the natural eye, so most people are unaware that they even exist. TRUE/FALSE

5. Satan's attack against people are:

    a. haphazard
    b. unplanned
    c. coincidental
    d. strategic

6. Putting on the Full Armor of God means to be fully armed with the _____.

7. Knowing a lot of scripture IS/IS NOT enough to win the victory over the enemy's tactics.

8. "Ephesians 6 gives us an illustration of *dressing ourselves in spiritual garments*. It's a picture of application."

    Why must we put on the Full Armor in the order given?

9. When you've lost confidence in yourself, you can renew your faith in God. TRUE/FALSE

10. When you outgrow the identity crisis, you will outgrow the _____ _____.

11. Why is the Sword of the Spirit the last piece of armor mentioned?

12. Write this sentence below: *"Spiritual and emotional growth take time. I will give myself the time I need to embrace the process."*

🔥 🔥 🔥

BONUS QUESTION: The Freedom Class details putting on the Full Armor of God to attain lasting emotional freedom through *spiritual and emotional growth*.

Why do you think EMOTIONAL GROWTH is necessary? Why not just SPIRITUAL GROWTH?

CHAPTER ELEVEN

The Kingdom of God

NO SERIOUS DISCUSSION OF SPIRITUAL MATTERS would be complete without including at least some mention of the Kingdom of God. This intriguing topic is particularly relevant to The Freedom Class, with its focus on *identity*. We don't have time for an extensive study of the Kingdom, due to the depth of the content, but I will often refer to Kingdom principles. So allow me to take a moment and highlight some basics about the Kingdom of God so we'll all be on the same page.

An elementary knowledge of the Kingdom of God is essential for believers. In fact, Jesus spent most of His ministry time on Earth teaching His disciples all about the Kingdom of God, Kingdom principles, and how to operate by Kingdom law. From the time Jesus began His ministry until the time He ascended back into Heaven, He talked about the Kingdom, the Kingdom, the Kingdom. When Jesus said He was going about His Father's business, He meant He was going about Kingdom business.

Jesus stressed the importance of putting Kingdom business first.

> *But seek first the kingdom of God and his righteousness, and all these things will be added to you.*
> *—Matthew 6:33*

To begin, let's establish that there is a very real place called *Heaven*. It's a spiritual place, not a natural one. However, to label Heaven as a *spiritual* place does not mean that it isn't real. Spiritual entities are more than just concepts of thought. *Spiritual realities* and *natural realities* exist on different planes of reality, yet they both do exist. They are both real. You might consider these different planes of reality as separate *dimensions*. According to *Smithsonian Magazine*, there is the "mind-bending possibility" that multiple dimensions exist in our universe. (That does without a doubt blow my mind.) However you choose to look at it, God is a Spirit, and He exists in the spiritual realm, the highest dimension. Things of the spiritual realm often trump things of the natural, but things of the natural never trump the spiritual.

The realm of Heaven is called the *Kingdom of Heaven*. The expansion of that Kingdom to the Earth is referred to as the *Kingdom of God*. Although there is a specific difference, often the two terms are used interchangeably. However, Heaven is where the actual throne of God is, so you might say it's the homeland. God's Kingdom, both in Heaven and on Earth, is also called the *Kingdom of light*.

God operates His government over Heaven and all creation as a kingdom. A true kingdom is owned, operated, and run by a *monarchy*, a supreme power usually comprised of a royal family, with a king (or queen) as its head.

As we progress through the series, we will often discuss the characteristics and qualities of the Kingdom of God as they apply to our journey. There are some facets of Kingdom principles that pertain more to our study than others. For now, let's settle on five fundamental truths about the Kingdom of God.

⸻ ♦ ♦ ♦ ⸻

1) Every kingdom has a king.

The King is Sovereign; that is, He has absolute power. Our God, the Father of our Lord Jesus Christ, sits on the throne of Heaven. The Bible describes Jesus Christ as King of kings and Lord of lords (1 Timothy 6:15, Revelation 17:14, Revelation 19:16).

2) Every kingdom has a territory.

Heaven is the homeland of the Kingdom of God. But long ago, God began expanding His Kingdom to the Earth. He created mankind to be His ambassadors—much like a regent sent to rule and exercise authority in the king's place. That Kingdom expansion is continuing today.

As children of God and subjects of His Kingdom, mankind (both male and female) was created in the image of God and commissioned to bring to the Earth the culture of Heaven. This included the customs, the laws, the manners, the observances, the practices, the form and formalities, the policies, even the very atmosphere of Heaven. To empower humans to accomplish this great assignment, God granted them *dominion*, or rulership, over the Earth. Humans still possess that dominion today.

When Jesus taught the disciples how to pray, He confirmed the original assignment. "Your kingdom come, your will be done, on earth as it is in heaven" (Matthew 6:10) is clarification that Kingdom policies are still in effect on the Earth.

3) Every kingdom has citizens or subjects.

As a believer, you are a citizen of the Kingdom of God right now. You don't have to wait until you die and go to Heaven to gain your citizenship. The Kingdom of God is here and now, and you're a part of it (Philippians 3:20).

4) Every kingdom has a constitution.

The constitution of the Kingdom of God is the Bible (God's Word). This constitution is supreme law. It defines the principles of the Kingdom and outlines specific commands for citizens. These include instructions on how to operate in the Kingdom, and specifies obligations and privileges. It also contains requirements for attaining citizenship in the Kingdom of God—that is, to accept Jesus Christ as Lord.

5) Every kingdom has laws.

The Kingdom of God has laws, and these are known as *spiritual laws*. Spiritual laws apply in the spirit realm, just as natural laws (like gravity) apply in the natural realm. Although unseen to the natural eye, spiritual laws are just as real as natural laws, perhaps even more so. Spiritual laws do not submit to natural laws, but natural laws do at times submit to spiritual laws. When this happens, the result is commonly known as a *miracle*.

In a kingdom, whatever the king says becomes law. Spiritual laws are truths from the heart of God. They are eternal and never change because God never changes. Spiritual laws are final and absolute, and cannot be broken. God is a God of laws. If you don't like abiding by laws, you'll have trouble getting along with the Lord. (Laws and rules are not the same thing.)

One spiritual law is that *God's Word is irrefutable*. God's Word never changes. When God speaks, He always fulfills His Word. He will never go back on His Word, no matter the consequence. *Never*.

SPIRITUAL LAW #1:
God's Word is irrefutable. He will not go back on His Word.

The Kingdom of God operates *legally*. That is, it works according to spiritual law. God is the executor of divine law. He will not lie, steal, or do anything contrary to His flawless nature.

Concerning Kingdom topics, our focus during this study will be on spiritual law. *Possessing a basic understanding of spiritual law can change your life*. I strongly urge you to pay special attention to the spiritual laws which are highlighted throughout the series. Working with spiritual laws, rather than against them, can make your life immensely easier.

Another spiritual law is that *the Kingdom of God is everlasting*. It cannot be changed or altered. It is eternal. (Psalm 145:13).

SPIRITUAL LAW #2:
The Kingdom of God is everlasting.

Jesus had some interesting things to say about the Kingdom of God. One day the religious leaders of Jesus' day asked Him when the Kingdom of God would come. (They were expecting a military takeover.) His answer was not what they expected.

> *Now when He was asked by the Pharisees when the kingdom of God would come, He answered them and said, "The kingdom of God does not come with observation; nor will they say, 'See here!' or 'See there!' For indeed, the kingdom of God is within you."*
> **Luke 17:20–21 (NKJV)**

The Kingdom of God is within you.

This revelation is a game changer. If the Kingdom of God is *within* us, then all that we need—all that the world needs—is at hand. *Our hand.* That puts a little responsibility on us, doesn't it?

When I read this verse, it makes me want to know more about this Kingdom. The best way to study the Kingdom of God is with the Kingdom's law book in hand. The Bible is the book that holds all the information we have about the Kingdom of God. By studying the Word of God, we can discover God's way of doing things. We can learn about what God has done; what is important to Him; what He likes and dislikes; what He demands from His children; what He purposes for His people. Your own experience in prayer, your spiritual journey, and your relationship with the Lord will teach you a lot about the Kingdom as well. By studying the Kingdom of God, you will come to know more about the King.

The Kingdom of God is a fascinating topic. For those who wish to learn more, I highly recommend the book *Principles of the Kingdom of God* by Dr. Myles Munroe.

> **By studying the Word of God, we can discover God's way of doing things.**

A War Between Kingdoms

We've talked a lot about battles and armor and such. For there to be a war, there must be at least two opposing sides. As it turns out, there are.

The Kingdom of God has an enemy: the kingdom of darkness. Its king and ruler is Satan, the archenemy of God and Heaven and all mankind. This devil is not some make-believe monster with a red suit and forked tail, but a very real spiritual presence with tremendous influence.

Satan was created as an angelic being named Lucifer. He was a worship leader in Heaven, designed with musical instruments built into his body. Lucifer was exceedingly gifted and very beautiful. One interesting thing about Lucifer is that he was one of only three anointed cherubs, the other two Michael and Gabriel. This fact gives him an unmistakable distinction.

We don't know the time frame involved in the course of events that chronicled the life of the archangel Lucifer and his eventual fall from Heaven. It could have been eons or millions of years; but then, time does not exist in Heaven, so those events cannot be measured according to earthly standards. We do know that Lucifer lived his heavenly existence basking in the light and magnificence of the presence of Almighty God. As one of the anointed cherubs, perhaps he had engaged countless conversations with the Most High. What we do know about Lucifer can be referenced in Ezekiel 28:12–17, Isaiah 14:12–15, and Luke 10:18.

At some point, Lucifer began to direct the heavenly worship toward himself. We can be sure that Lucifer knew the spiritual laws of Heaven very well, but as he exalted himself in pride, he began to try to bend those laws. He should have known better.

Eventually, Lucifer was thrown out of Heaven for attempting to usurp God's throne—but not before he started a war in Heaven and won the loyalty of one-third of the angels. With his followers, Lucifer—now called Satan—was cast down to the Earth, which then became his territory. The Bible refers to Satan as the "god of this world" (2 Corinthians 4:4). He does not have a domain in Heaven or on any other planet. It appears that the kingdom of darkness is relegated to the Earth.

> *For we do not wrestle against flesh and blood, but against the rulers, against the authorities, against the cosmic powers over this present darkness, against the spiritual forces of evil in the heavenly places.*
> —**Ephesians 6:12**

From this scripture, the phrases "cosmic powers" and "in the heavenly places" suggest the spiritual kingdom of darkness exists in the atmospheric realms of the Earth.

Sin reigns supreme in the kingdom of darkness, its mission to kill, steal, and destroy (John 10:10). Satan desires to see the culture of hell manifested onto the Earth. *For the record, the kingdom of darkness is not and never was equal to the Kingdom of God.* The kingdom of darkness is an inferior kingdom, just as its king is an inferior king.

There is a very real battle going on between the forces of good and evil. The devil knows he's no match for God because he is a created being, on the level with Michael and Gabriel—but never on the level with God. However, that fact has not deterred his pursuit of power. You'd think once he was kicked out of Heaven, he'd tuck his tail and hide somewhere—but no, Satan wants to build his own kingdom.

This is the shocking news: *Satan wants you for his kingdom*. His real argument is not with you, it's with God—but he has created a vicious campaign to win you over, and he'll go to all lengths to accomplish that mission. Why? Satan wants you for his kingdom because you are made in the image of God! You have tremendous powers of choice and creativity, which lend themselves very well to building kingdoms.

You are a kingdom builder.

> **More than anything else you will ever do or become in your life, you are primarily a kingdom builder.**

Mankind's great purpose is to expand the Kingdom of God on the Earth. God has granted His children collectively and individually all the tools, gifts, talents, intelligence, and creativity needed to accomplish that divine assignment. More than anything else you will ever do or become in your life, you are primarily a *kingdom builder*. However, things are a bit more complicated now than they were at the beginning. The waters are muddied. Because now the kingdom builders—that's you and me—have to choose between kingdoms.

The two kingdoms are both in the business of expanding. Both are recruiting. As a kingdom builder, you have the choice of which territory you will help build—but you don't get the choice of *whether* you'll build. You must build! Your creative kingdom-building abilities will be used to expand one kingdom or the other: the Kingdom of God, or the kingdom of darkness.

You've been drafted. Like it or not, you're now a major player in the epic battle of the universe. You'll either help to bring the Kingdom of God to the Earth . . . or you'll help to bring the kingdom of darkness to the Earth. It is impossible to be neutral in this battle.

CHAPTER ELEVEN WORKBOOK

THE KINGDOM OF GOD

---

1. From the time Jesus began His ministry until the time He ascended back into Heaven, Jesus talked about the _____, the _____, the _____.

2. Write out Matthew 6:33:

3. Every kingdom has:

    a. a king/queen
    b. territory
    c. citizens/subjects
    d. a constitution
    e. laws
    f. all of the above

4. What is Spiritual Law #1?

5. What is Spiritual Law #2?

6. Write out Luke 17:20–21:

7. According to the above verse (Question #6), what did Jesus mean when He said that the Kingdom of God is within you?

8. By studying the Bible, we can learn:

    a. God's way of doing things
    b. what God has done
    c. what is important to God
    d. what God likes and dislikes
    e. what the Lord demands from His children
    f. what God purposes for His people
    g. all of the above

9. Write out Ephesians 6:12:

10. "Satan desires to see the culture of hell manifested on the Earth."

    What evidence of this can you see in our world today?

11. The kingdom of darkness is not and never was _____ to the Kingdom of God.

12. "More than anything else you will ever do or become in your life, you are primarily a KINGDOM BUILDER."

    Why do you think the devil wants you for his kingdom?

🔥 🔥 🔥

BONUS QUESTION: What can you do TODAY to expand the Kingdom of God on the Earth?

CHAPTER TWELVE

The Power of Choice

IN BATTLES THROUGHOUT HISTORY, THERE HAVE AT TIMES been an area of battlefield called "no man's land." This strip of land is neutral ground—an unoccupied, unclaimed, and often disputed area between armies. In the spiritual realm, however, there is no neutral ground. There is no area called "no man's land." Wherever and whatever you build, it will be on territory firmly within either the Kingdom of God or the kingdom of darkness. There's no third option.

Satan wants you to help him build his kingdom. It's possible to do that even without realizing it. This is where *your ability to choose* carries substantial weight.

Let's go ahead and recognize another important spiritual law right now:

SPIRITUAL LAW #3:
Every person is created as a free moral agent with the power of choice.

The Lord doesn't want an army of robots in humanity. That's why He created mankind as *free moral agents* who can think and make decisions for themselves. People have the responsibility to make moral judgments and be held accountable for their actions. This is the phenomenal *power of choice*. The gift of personal jurisdiction creates an autonomy of independent thought, which is profound in its significance. Even when one cannot control their circumstances, they can choose how they will respond.

When the Lord created the first humans, He placed them on the Earth in a sinless world. There was no disease, no poverty, no relationship issues. It was a perfect setup. But even then, Adam and Eve were tempted to reach outside God's grace to attain selfish desires. Within their garden home was a tree, the fruit of which they were not to eat. If they did, God said they would die. The tree was left unguarded, available to the first couple as a test of their will and obedience.

We know the story, how Satan deceived the woman and enticed her to eat the fruit. She ate, and she gave the fruit to Adam, and he ate too. Through that event, known as *the fall of man*, sin entered the world and the culture of hell began to invade and expand. The fight for territory between the kingdoms began.

> **Even when one cannot control their circumstances, they can choose how they will respond.**

The decisions that led to the fall had huge implications on the lives of the first humans and those of future generations. Some might wonder why the Lord would give such potential power to His human children, knowing what they could do with it. But we serve a bold and fearless God, and this is God's way of doing things. The Lord granted Adam and Eve the power of choice, even when He knew they would choose wrongly.

Our God doesn't make anyone serve Him. There are no slaves or forced labor in His Kingdom. To function effectively in the Kingdom of God, one must be a willing participant. This is the heart of the Father. The Lord desires for His children to voluntarily align themselves with the Kingdom of Heaven—not by force, but through personal choice and often by sacrifice.

The following verse is a narrative of how the Lord once presented a significant choice to the Israelites. They had just escaped the oppression of Egypt only to find themselves homeless in a new and strange wilderness. God had an exciting future for these people, but He needed them to get in covenant with Him to fulfill His purposes. He would not force them to comply, but He appealed to their good sense and gave them the option to decline.

> *I call heaven and earth to witness against you today,*
> *that I have set before you life and death, blessing and curse.*
> *Therefore choose life, that you and your offspring may live . . .*
> *—Deuteronomy 30:19*

For the Israelites, it was life or death, blessing or curse. There was no middle road, no alternate path. The God of Heaven was calling the descendants of Abraham into a covenant with Him in which He would be their God and they would be His people. It would be a covenant for all time, one which would influence the souls of all people everywhere. The stakes were high. But still, they had to choose. God would not choose for them.

Thankfully, they chose life! They willingly entered into a covenant with Heaven, which stands to this day. Through that arrangement came the Messiah, Jesus Christ, and a new covenant which offers salvation to all. The select favor as God's chosen people, which once belonged only to the Hebrew people, is now available to "whosoever will."

God granted the gift of choice to all humanity, knowing that people might use it for all the wrong reasons. They might use it to build the wrong kingdom—and, unfortunately, they often do. But through the power of the anointing, men and women of God can oppose Satan's efforts, frustrate the kingdom of darkness, and weaken the power of the enemy. Specifically, believers can bring the Kingdom of God to the Earth.

That is why you are a personal threat to the devil.

Satan is afraid of believers because he knows they have access to the Kingdom of God. His fight is not really with humans; it's with God. But he hates God's children because they have the supernatural ability to bring God's Kingdom to his domain. The devil cannot operate in the

Kingdom of God. He is powerless there, because the Kingdom of God is a Kingdom of light, and he thrives only in the darkness. I believe that's one reason why he works so hard to hinder believers in their walk with Christ.

Satan's first attack on a child of God is *about their identity*. The devil is well aware that if believers ever find out who they are, he's in trouble. Because when a child of God realizes their true worth and gets a grip on their real spiritual identity—that they are one with Christ, full of power and authority—then they realize they have a choice. They don't have to settle for less than full-blown joy and victory, because they know they have access to all the power of Heaven, that the Kingdom of God is within them. They'll begin to operate in remarkable spiritual strength, building the Kingdom of God, manifesting the kind of love that changes things.

The devil wants to stop people before they ever get started. Through the use of a heart bondage, he manages to create an identity crisis early in childhood. His full intention is to keep God's children confused about who they are throughout their lifetime so they never figure it out—and that's *all God's children*, both the saved and the unsaved. The tactics of the kingdom of darkness are aimed at all humans, not just Christians. Satan wants to prevent believers from being effective for the Kingdom of God, and he wants to prevent unbelievers from becoming believers.

> **You have a say in what you allow in your life, even in your destiny to some degree.**

But knowledge is power, and now you know. You know about heart bondages and spiritual chains, and how the enemy uses them to kill, steal, and destroy. But you also know about some other things: For one, you don't have to accept a life stunted by shame and hopelessness because of enemy threats. You don't have to tolerate a marginal existence choked by fear, condemned by accusation, trapped in a wilderness of isolation. You have a say in what you allow in your life, even in your destiny to some degree. You can choose life—*abundant life*—because you have the power of choice.

Spiritual Warfare

Attaining emotional freedom is, in the strictest terms, a *deliverance*. To receive a deliverance and the ensuing freedom from a heart bondage requires *spiritual warfare*. That term can mean different things to different people. But sometimes "spiritual warfare" can take on a particular hue when associated with inner healing or deliverance. It's not uncommon for deliverance ministries to practice the laying on of hands, the calling out and rebuking of demons, and other aggressive tactics. Often just the mention of deliverance sounds spooky to some people.

If you're getting nervous, you can relax. We will not be practicing any of those types of deliverance methods in this series. While there is indeed a place and time for such practices, we will not be going there. It's simply not necessary. In The Freedom Class, we are dealing with generational curses, not demonic possession. Whether or not you believe in aggressive deliverance methods, attaining freedom from a heart bondage does not require that kind of approach.

Let's look again at what the Apostle Paul had to say about spiritual warfare:

> *For though we walk in the flesh, we do not war according to the flesh. For the weapons of our warfare are not carnal but mighty in God for pulling down strongholds, casting down arguments and every high thing that exalts itself against the knowledge of God, bringing every thought into captivity to the obedience of Christ . . .*
> 2 Corinthians 10:3–5 (NKJV)

This passage makes a strong statement about the nature of our struggle. First and foremost, don't miss the fact that we're in a war. It's a war all right, but not a natural war; it's a *spiritual war*. These tools of the enemy (strongholds) are devices that are spiritual in nature, and they must be demolished the same way they were put on: with *spiritual warfare*. So since we are in a spiritual war, the weapons we need to win must be spiritual weapons, not natural ones—and according to the above scripture, we have them! We have weapons at hand that are "not carnal but mighty in God," weapons specifically for *pulling down strongholds, casting down arguments, and bringing every thought into captivity.*

- **pulling down strongholds**
- **casting down arguments**
- **bringing every thought into captivity**

The Apostle Paul calls these the *weapons of our warfare*. But what exactly are these weapons, and where do we get them?

Look again at the warrior of Ephesians 6. He is a warrior dressed for battle, specifically a *spiritual battle*. The Ephesians 6 passage states that we are not fighting a natural battle of "flesh and blood," but we are warring against spiritual entities—rulers, authorities, cosmic powers, and "spiritual forces of evil in the heavenly places." That, my friend, is a *spiritual fight*.

Second Corinthians 10:3–5 and Ephesians 6 are talking about the same spiritual battle. Not a natural battle, but a spiritual one.

The weapons we need for the spiritual battle of 2 Corinthians 10:3–5 are on the warrior of Ephesians 6. By putting on the Full Armor of God and incorporating effective, fervent prayer, we go to battle against the powers of darkness and engage in spiritual warfare that gets results.

Spiritual battles do not respond to natural tactics. That is why the power of positive thinking and other systems of thought for improved mental health and happiness, although helpful, will not dislodge a heart bondage. Such practices might somewhat alleviate the Serious Symptoms, but the foundational brokenness will override any conscious attempt to overcome it through natural means. The enemy waged spiritual warfare against you when he installed the heart bondage, and you are going to have to fight a spiritual battle to break those chains.

Spiritual warfare is both a necessity and a privilege for the mature believer—and that's all believers, not just church leaders. It's for you and me. Our God has given us weapons—not "according to the flesh," but spiritual ones. They're given to us to use, and you can do it through

Spiritual Law

Spiritual Law #1: God's Word is irrefutable.
  The Lord never goes back on His Word.

  Psalm 119:89   1 Peter 1:25
  Isaiah 40:8   Matthew 24:35

Spiritual Law #2: The Kingdom of God is everlasting.
  God sits on the throne of Heaven. There is no contender for His throne; there never was, and there never will be.

  Psalm 45:6   Lamentations 5:19
  Daniel 4:3   2 Peter 1:11

Spiritual Law #3: Every person is created in the image of God as a free moral agent with the power of choice.

  Genesis 1:26   Deuteronomy 30:19
  Acts 5:29   Ephesians 4:22-24

* This short list of spiritual laws is composed for the purposes of this study and is by no means a comprehensive list. There are indeed many spiritual laws. However, I have chosen these three to begin our conversation because they embody foundational principles that help us understand the Kingdom of God and our relationship to it. Additional spiritual laws will be added to this list in the following volumes of the Armor Series.

the power of the Spirit! I am going to show you how. Emotional freedom is as much a promise to you as it is to any other believer.

Jesus Christ has already won the battle for your freedom. When you follow His lead *precisely the way the Word of God says,* you are guaranteed a victory. If there ever was a fixed fight, this is it!

CHAPTER TWELVE WORKBOOK

THE POWER OF CHOICE

1. In the spiritual realm, there is no neutral ground. You must choose between kingdoms. TRUE/FALSE

2. What is Spiritual Law #3:

3. Describe a FREE MORAL AGENT.

4. To function in the Kingdom of God effectively, one must be a willing _____.

5. Write out Deuteronomy 30:19:

6. In the scripture above (Question #5), the two choices God gave the Israelites were _____ or _____.

7. "God granted the gift of choice to all humanity, knowing that people might use it for all the wrong reasons."

   Have you ever used your gifts/talents/anointing for the wrong reasons? If so, explain.

   How can you change that to building the Kingdom of God?

8. The devil wants to keep God's children confused:
   a. just till they grow up
   b. as long as they are serving God
   c. until they turn 40
   d. throughout their lifetime

9. Write this sentence: *I can choose the abundant life because I have the power of choice.*

10. Attaining emotional freedom involves spiritual warfare. TRUE/FALSE

11. Write out 2 Corinthians 10:3–5:

12. According to the above scripture (#11), the weapons of our warfare are for:

    a. pulling down strongholds
    b. casting down arguments
    c. bringing every thought into captivity to the obedience of Christ
    d. all the above

BONUS QUESTION: Why are you a personal threat to the devil?

CHAPTER THIRTEEN

A Measure of Grace

THE FREEDOM CLASS IS A POWERFUL AND EFFECTIVE course which leads to lasting emotional freedom. However, The Freedom Class is not the answer to all life's challenges. There are concerns which The Freedom Class cannot resolve, and you should know what they are so that your expectations will be realistic. The following four points describe what The Freedom Class is not:

1) The seven steps presented in The Freedom Class are not static, stoic procedures.

The process presented in The Freedom Class is not a formula. The path to freedom is portrayed as a series of steps, but they are more than a list of "dos and don'ts."

Nothing in this series is religious. However, the content of the class is relatively structured. Each of the steps represents a portion of truth that can stand alone, and as such can be viewed as a separate message. But the progression necessary for freedom from a heart bondage requires emotional growth, which involves engaging the entire series. The steps must be approached in a particular order. It's a sequential work and a deeply personal one.

Occasionally I see students in The Freedom Class who don't make progress. When that happens, it's usually because they've neglected to engage the material as an exercise. Typically there is a lack of commitment as well. Freedom warriors must be courageous enough to do whatever is necessary for transformational change. That involves *active and honest participation by the believer*.

2) The Freedom Class is not a magic wand.

Attaining emotional freedom is a life-changing event. It is not, however, a cure-all. Emotional freedom is not a panacea for all life's ills.

Everyone has problems in this life because life is like that. Jesus said there would be trouble in this world (John 16:33). Even those who managed to escape childhood without emotional injury will still have their share of trouble.

But life is generally more difficult for those with a heart bondage. Shame and hopelessness are not precursors for an abundant life. However, *all your problems are not and never were singularly due to your issues from childhood*.

After you receive your freedom, you will still have some challenges to face. You'll still have problems. Some of them may be the same old problems you have now. *But shame and hopelessness will not be among them.*

3) The Freedom Class is not a counseling tool.

The Freedom Class is not a counseling tool, and I am not a counselor—professionally, or in any other capacity. I do not use any professional psychological methods, as indeed I don't possess any, nor do I rely on any deliverance techniques used by any other ministry or organization. My techniques, if indeed they can be called such, are entirely based on scripture and my own revelation of understanding as revealed by the Holy Spirit's work in my life.

Students will find that in this study, very little attention is awarded to feelings. Even in the accompanying Workbook, the impact of emotions is all but absent, except for a short section in Endurance (Step 4). This is not an oversight, nor is it due to inconsideration toward anyone's feelings. It's a measure I deliberately employed because the interminable expression of feelings doesn't usually solve anything. God Himself doesn't seem to put much stock in feelings. Our God is an action God who says *go* and *do*, not *if you feel like it*. I've been very careful to replicate my own journey and offer the same experience to all who would follow that path. During the course of my journey, the Lord never seemed to consider my feelings to be a significant factor.

4) The freedom process is not complicated.

Spiritual and emotional growth takes work. As you progress through the steps in The Freedom Class, you'll be challenged with a series of decisions, some of which may make you a bit uncomfortable. Some of the content may make you uncomfortable as well. But no one can do the work for you; you have to do it. It helps to remember that nothing extraordinary ever happened in anyone's comfort zone. So we really shouldn't be overly concerned about our comfort level if we want to experience life-changing spiritual and emotional growth. There is such a thing as growing pains.

The good news is, you don't have to figure out how to attain your freedom or labor over a deliverance. That's the thing about this message that seems almost too good to be true for some people. It is supremely uncomplicated. There is an emotional rebirth to be won, and all you have to do is engage the process. Read the material, complete the Workbook exercises, comply with the Word of God, and participate honestly. *Can anything be that simple?* Yes, it's that simple!

Of course, *simple* doesn't always mean *easy*. But it does mean *doable*. Students of The Freedom Class are consistently astonished by the simplicity of the process. They express their amazement, even as they describe the internal changes they sense. As one person said, "You'd think it would be harder."

And that's just like God, isn't it? His Word is always simple. If it's complicated, it's probably not God.

Much of the content in The Freedom Class you may have heard before, especially if you're a seasoned believer. But there is something about this teaching of the Full Armor of God that is different. Perhaps it's in the order of application. I just know that it works. It's God's way of doing things, God's way of dismantling tools of the enemy. It's God's way of setting people free!

Back to Choice Again

God created us, this species of mankind, *in His image*. Our ability to make decisions is one way we are most like Him. The Lord allows us to participate in formulating our own lives, establishing our personal values, determining our own greatness, and to a considerable degree, forging our own destinies. This characteristic sets us apart from the rest of creation and most defines the image of God in us: *the power to choose*. Mankind lives according to a free will that is a gift from God and a notable characteristic of the Creator Himself.

I am always amazed when I think of all that God invested in people. When He granted mankind the power of choice, the Lord had to know there was tremendous potential for disaster. That seems to me like a risky business! And frankly, it was a risk. But our God is a God of faith. So along with that gift of choice, He invested in humans a measure of grace. Grace cannot exist without choice, because our will is reciprocally related with the ability to choose—and grace is not necessary where there is no weakness. God knew that His human children would fall, but despite the ensuing sin nature, His grace would be enough.

The amazing thing about your power of choice is—well, *the power*.

When it comes to your life, God allows you to make the call. He will honor your choices over His own. He will do this, even when He is not pleased with your choices. God will not stop you even when you're making the worst decisions of your life.

> *This characteristic sets us apart from the rest of creation and most defines the image of God in us: the power to choose.*

There is a perfect purpose for your life. Whether or not that plan ever materializes is primarily up to you. You really can't blame God for the consequences of your own choices. If you make decisions that are contradictory to divine guidance, He will allow your will to trump His.

People sometimes wonder why the Lord allows certain things to happen. But perhaps the question we should be asking is, *Why are we allowing certain things to happen?* What are we allowing in our lives?

Truly, I say to you, whatever you bind on earth shall be bound in heaven, and whatever you loose on earth shall be loosed in heaven.
—Matthew 18:18

Whatever we "bind" or restrain in our lives, God will restrain. Whatever we allow, God will allow. Granted, some things are out of our direct control. But much of life is within our control.

At this moment, you have the power of choice over the brokenness that has attempted to redefine your identity and redirect your life. Will you allow it? Or will you choose to claim your victory over the darkness? There are only the two choices.

There was a day, on a Fourth of July weekend, when I stood in my laundry room and made a decision for change, for life. *For freedom.* I chose to turn from the fear and, though my knees were shaking, plunged headlong into a journey that would take me wondrous places I had never known. I used my power of choice that day to act in my own stead, fully aware that I had allowed the chaos, albeit unwittingly—but also aware that there was a window open for a second chance. *Another chance.* The landscape of my life stretched before me like a heap of ashes, reduced to a mere wisp by the flames of shame which had destroyed my entire life's work. *Burned to the ground.* But even then it was not too late. I still possessed the power of choice, and I could use that power for change. So I said no to the lies, no to the deception, no to the fear. When I said *no*, God said *no*, and it was over. For me, there was no going back, and I was in blissful agreement with Heaven: *God's way of doing things is the only way of doing things.*

I believe the Lord wants you to experience complete emotional freedom. I can say that with confidence, because I know what God's Word has to say about the matter. I know His nature. It's not the Lord's will that anyone is enslaved by chains of shame and hopelessness, which is nothing less than a wicked device contrived by the enemy for destruction and ruin. Freedom is for you, and it's for me; it's for every believer. That's why our God has provided a way out—a simple, time-tested process that leads to profound and lasting emotional freedom.

You can never defeat the power of darkness through natural efforts or means. You can, however, trust that God, the Maker of your soul, knows how to do that. He knows what it takes to defeat the enemy and bring victory to your situation—specifically, freedom from the bondage of shame and hopelessness placed upon your heart as a child. The method of putting on the Full Armor of God, as presented in The Freedom Class, is effective and powerful. The great Apostle Paul preached it, and his words still preach it from the pages of the Bible. It worked for me, and it will work for you. God's Word works every time!

Join me in The Freedom Class. *It's your choice!*

CHAPTER THIRTEEN WORKBOOK

A MEASURE OF GRACE

1. All your problems in life are not due to issues from childhood. TRUE/FALSE

2. God Himself doesn't seem to put much stock in feelings. Our God is an action God who says _____ and _____, not *if you feel like it.*

3. To successfully complete The Freedom Class, you should be concerned about:

    a. how long it takes
    b. what other people think about it
    c. your comfort level
    d. being offended by the material
    e. none of the above

4. If it's _____, it's probably not God.

5. Our ability to make decisions is one way we are most like God. TRUE/FALSE

6. When it comes to your life, God will:

    a. let you make the call
    b. make the decision for you
    c. get other people to decide
    d. wait and see what happens
    e. none of the above

7. Have you ever made any decisions about your life that you knew the Lord did not approve? List up to three below:

1. _____
2. _____
3. _____

8. Write out Matthew 18:18:

9. Do you believe God wants you to experience emotional freedom? Explain.

10. Write this sentence below: *I can trust that God, the Maker of my soul, knows what it takes to bring victory to my situation and set me free from emotional bondage.*

11. God is the God of:

    a. a second chance
    b. a third chance
    c. a fourth chance
    d. another chance

12. God's way of doing things is the only way of doing things.
    TRUE/FALSE

🔥 🔥 🔥

BONUS QUESTION: Perhaps you know someone who may receive hope through this book and Debbie's message of emotional freedom. Do you think you can share it with them? If so, complete the sentence below.

I can share this book with: _____.

CHAPTER FOURTEEN

The Freedom Class Online

THE FREEDOM CLASS IS A SEVEN-STEP CURRICULUM that helps believers attain emotional freedom by dealing with issues from childhood. The content is presented in the four-volume *Armor Series*, of which this book, *Instead of Shame*, is Book One. With the focus on scriptural applications to resolve personal concerns, an accompanying Workbook is available as a companion to the Series. (Components of the Workbook are located in all four volumes.)

The Freedom Class also offers an online classroom that serves as an assistant to the primary teaching material provided in the Armor Series. On the site is everything necessary to begin and complete the course: access to the seven steps; the Workbook; and various means of support. Through instructional video, webinars, and other avenues of technology, The Freedom Class Online provides encouragement and guidance designed to help students navigate the seven steps outlined in the curriculum.

The online class is delightfully convenient for students of freedom. Wherever one is in the Series, they can jump in and participate in a homework session or access a video. The built-in flexibility enables students to proceed at their own speed. Assistance is available and posted for all seven steps and the corresponding Workbook. I strongly encourage all freedom warriors to take advantage of the support avenues offered online.

Last but certainly not least is the option of local group meetings. Often students of The Freedom Class wish to join with others and enjoy the camaraderie of group support. Participating in a group of like-minded people with a common purpose provides an opportunity to dispel the feelings of isolation that is so characteristic of brokenness. You'll have the chance to share your story and encourage someone else, even as you receive encouragement for your journey. It's a great way to engage the Series and can be incredibly helpful with the Workbook applications. Guidelines for local group meetings are on the The Freedom Class website.

Also on the site are testimonials, some available products, and suggested schedules for reading and completing the course. Visit the site at

thefreedomclass.org

Your Personal Invitation

At the beginning of this book, I said that if I'd had someone offer me a way out of my brokenness at eighteen years of age, I would have jumped at the chance. You have that chance right now. Today you have what is known as a *golden opportunity*. And the timing is perfect! It's a time when you can reach up and grab hold of the promises of God and bring them down to Earth.

The very thing you've become discouraged about—that weight of shame and hopelessness—can be over. Perhaps you've made a deal with yourself to live in the shadows of the past because you thought you couldn't do anything about it. Or maybe you've reasoned with yourself that it's just a part of life or a facet of your personality. But brokenness is not who you are. It only feels that way because it has become familiar. You may have given up in the past, but today is a new day. It's time to reach up and believe for the impossible.

Leading others to emotional freedom is my greatest pleasure because it is precisely what God did for me. In this book and the following volumes that comprise the Armor Series, I have been careful to duplicate my own experience just as it happened so others can walk through the process *exactly as I did*. I have not tweaked it or altered the process in any way.

In The Freedom Class, I will take you by the hand and walk you through a process that can change your life. It is a journey that leads to lasting emotional freedom. I have traveled this path, and I can show you how to travel this path. As they say, I have been there and done that. I can, without a doubt, lead you to freedom.

But I cannot set you free. *Only God can set you free.*

I believe you are called to freedom. It is the nature of God within us to live unencumbered by the weight of bondage, to resist limitations on our hope, to connect unhindered to the creative power within us. It is not God's will that any remain bound. Jesus said that He came to "proclaim liberty to the captives" and "to set at liberty those who are oppressed" (Luke 4:18).

Dare to believe! Let your faith soar as you answer the call to hope in Jesus Christ. He is the Deliverer, the Healer, the greatest Freedom Warrior ever. It's no coincidence that God brought me through my own journey and then gave me the map to the journey after the fact. He showed me the path I had walked, a path of truth and light, but it was not just for me that He did that. My freedom was for me, but the map was for you. *This message is for you.*

Consider this your personal invitation to The Freedom Class. This is your time, your day. Your opportunity!

Take my hand, and let's begin. As we take that first step together, our focus will be on:

- God, our Deliverer
- Jesus Christ, our Salvation
- the Holy Spirit, our Comforter and Guide.

Our focus will be on the Truth of God's Word, as He leads us to *freedom in Christ Jesus!*

And now...

JOIN ME IN

The Freedom Class!

www.thefreedomclass.org

ACKNOWLEDGMENTS

I AM IMMENSELY GRATEFUL TO PARTICIPANTS OF THE early Freedom Classes that served as my course development laboratory. What a pleasure and encouragement to meet every week with people who had faith in the message as well as the messenger. In those first meetings, the landscape of The Freedom Class took shape. Thank you for your kindness, steadfast participation, and faith in the message you embraced, which will now be available to many people through the Armor Series.

Thank you to all my pastors, former and present, including the late Rev Earl and Christine Johnson, Jerry and Elaine Ables, Brian and Kimberly Bohrer, Terry and Dorcas Maris, John and LaNell Miller, and Eddie and Sherri Cupples. The world is a better place because of you.

And many thanks to the publishing professionals: Marilyn Price of Broken Arrow, Oklahoma, Ryan Scheife of Mayfly Design, and Marly Cornell.

And finally, my enormous and loving thanks to my family for their unfailing support and encouragement.

ABOUT THE AUTHOR

DEBBIE WALLACE has a BA in Mass Communication from Southern Arkansas University in Magnolia, Arkansas. She has worked in radio, as a Realtor, and as a hotel general manager. She is a pianist and has served as a worship leader in various churches. Debbie has a personal story that has proven relatable to many. She uses her testimony as a speaker and podcaster who is passionate about matters of faith and spiritual development. She has three daughters and four grandchildren. Debbie lives in Jackson, Tennessee.

COMING SOON!!!

Book Two in the Armor Series

Instead of Disgrace

The message is to get real and come as you are as Book Two approaches the concepts of Truth and Relationship with Jesus Christ as foundations to emotional health and well-being.

TRUTH

Part One: An Introduction to Truth

TRUTH: *The state or character of being true; the actual state of a matter; a standard or original. An ideal or fundamental reality apart from transcending perceived experience.*

The Beginning of Freedom

THE FIRST STEP IN THE JOURNEY TO EMOTIONAL FREEdom is **TRUTH.** Truth is the way things are according to the One who knows Truth and is absolute Truth: *Jesus!* Truth is not subject to human judgment, but it's about God's perspective.

Many people lie to themselves about their experiences in life and in their relationships in order to survive, literally hiding behind a mask of deception. Such was the case in my own life. We have all, at times, had trouble reconciling what we believe with what we see.

But there is a world of difference between Truth and evidence—and this is what we must come to know if we are to thrive instead of merely survive. If there is a gap between God's Word and our common realities—between the way things should be and the way things are—then we must know that the problem is with us. The problem is never with the divine, because God's character is flawless. His Word is the foundation of all Truth.

Truth is a vibrant, living force greater than any collection of facts. It is a teacher to that enlightened intelligence we call *understanding*, without which there is not and never can be any real discovery in the heart of man. Truth is the way out of our dilemma, because embracing Truth is the beginning of freedom.

The day came when I knew I had to get real with myself and close the gap between my ideals and my realities. I had lied to myself and allowed unbridled turbulence in my life by excusing the behavior of those around me. I had lived to please critical people who can never be pleased, bearing the responsibility of the behavior of others, thinking I was acting in love. I had it all backward! We can never be responsible for the behavior of others, only for ourselves. I had been true to everyone but myself.

This first step in your journey will prompt you to take a long, hard look at yourself. Genuine introspection requires both an acknowledgment of your strengths and a face-to-face confrontation with some unpleasant company residing in your soul in the form of memories and past hurts, failures, regrets, and disappointments. Real self-examination requires complete transparency, honesty, and openness. As you peel back the layers, the essence of Truth will reveal itself in unexpected ways.

The key word associated with Truth is *courage*. It takes courage to *get real*, especially concerning deeply ingrained perceptions. But as you embrace Truth, you will expose and abandon the lies you have allowed yourself to believe to survive and explain things that made no sense. At the same time, you will learn to apply Truth to those areas once misguided by deception. Words associated with Truth are *authenticity*, *genuineness*, *honesty*, and *transparency*.

My breakthrough came when I realized my situation was not about the external influences. It was about me. I had to surrender the lies and fully embrace God's truth: that Jesus Christ is more than enough, and I never was. That I could not resolve my inner conflict of broken identity in my own strength, but that Christ, and Christ alone, is the Healer of hearts. An encounter with Truth changed the course of my life.

And it will change yours.

~

Made in the USA
Middletown, DE
01 April 2025